DOCTOR
LAWYER
ENGINEER

Brennan,

Thanks you so much for your support in bringing this book to life!

My journey in Seattle was an important chapter in my life and I am so grateful to have had your support and encouragement throughout.

I really do admire your hustle and precision and high level of productivity, and I hope that you enjoy the read!

~Nnamdi

DOCTOR LAWYER ENGINEER

HOW TO PURSUE YOUR DREAMS WITHOUT GIVING YOUR PARENTS A HEART ATTACK.

NNAMDI NWAEZEAPU

NEW DEGREE PRESS

DOCTOR LAWYER ENGINEER

How to pursue your dreams without giving your parents a heart attack.

ISBN 978-1-63676-616-4 *Paperback*

978-1-63676-288-3 *Kindle Ebook*

978-1-63676-289-0 *Ebook*

"We shall not cease from exploration
And the end of all our exploring
Will be to arrive where we started
And know the place for the first time.

—T.S. ELIOT, FOUR QUARTETS

CONTENTS

INTRODUCTION		11
PART 1.	**YOU ARE HERE.**	**17**
CHAPTER 1.	FOREIGN INVESTMENTS	19
CHAPTER 2.	SURVIVAL	29
CHAPTER 3.	MOTHERS OF TIGERS	39
CHAPTER 4.	PARENTING, PERFECTIONISM, AND PSYCHOPATHOLOGY	53
CHAPTER 5.	DEVELOPING YOUR INTERESTS	63
PART 2.	**POTENTIAL PATHS**	**71**
CHAPTER 6.	THE TALK	73
CHAPTER 7.	FINISHING THE RACE.	89
CHAPTER 8.	ACTING DIFFERENT	99
CHAPTER 9.	DIFFERENT PERSPECTIVES	109
PART 3.	**WALKING THE WALK**	**119**
CHAPTER 10.	UNLAWFULLY WEDDED	121
CHAPTER 11.	DO YOU REALLY WANT TO PURSUE YOUR DREAM?	131
CHAPTER 12.	THE IMPORTANCE OF HAVING A PLAN	143
CHAPTER 13.	HOW TO CHOOSE THE RIGHT PLAN	153
CHAPTER 14.	CONCLUSION	159
ACKNOWLEDGEMENTS		163
APPENDIX		165

To Mom & Dad.

INTRODUCTION

What does your dream life look like? Really take a moment here and actually try to visualize it. Seriously—stop and think before you keep reading.

Where would you live? What would the weather be like? How would you dress? How would you feel?

Two years ago, I had a clear vision for my dream life. I wanted to be a jet-setting, cold-shower-taking entrepreneur. I would live in an ultra-modern apartment in New York City and spend most of my days exploring and flying to new places, taking breaks to write and tend to my profitable business. I also would be in peak shape, make virtually no mistakes, and have an easygoing approach to life.

This vision was a stark contrast to my reality at the time. I had no plans of being on a jet anytime soon, and my showers were mostly hot. My apartment was *not* ultra-modern, and I spent most of my days inside experiencing existential anguish, taking breaks to study and write. I also was not in peak shape, made a lot of mistakes, and was the opposite of easygoing.

I was in the middle of my first year at Columbia Law School. And, as many people warned me prior to entering, it was hard. Law school involves a lot of reading and the classes are essentially designed to stress you out. But the difficulties of school really weren't my issue—I was no longer sure that I wanted to be a lawyer.

In my junior year of college, an internship at a big fancy law firm exposed me to the legal profession. I walked through a lobby made of marble every day, attended extravagant galas, and earned more than I had ever been paid in my life. After this amazing internship, I decided that I would become an attorney—not because I had any particular love for law, but simply because the profession seemed prestigious and I knew it would make my parents happy.

As a child of a Nigerian immigrant, I had been groomed from birth to place paramount importance on doing well in school. I also knew that becoming a doctor, lawyer, or engineer would make my dad extremely proud. In fact, as a kid, I recalled my younger brother being good at science and knew that he was likely going to become a doctor. My brother's success intensely motivated me to make my dad proud, too. Studying law felt like the best way to continue down the path of impressing my parents with my achievements and accolades.

Prior to entering law school, however, I went through your quintessential quarter-life crisis: high school sweetheart breaks your heart, yada yada yada—you get the idea. For the first time, the blinders that I had been wearing for the past five years had been knocked off, and I suddenly began to question my journey to become a lawyer. I had put so many of my other dreams on the back burner in the pursuit to attend law school and I began to worry that I was making a mistake.

Other people seemed to agree that my worries were justified. They told me, "Nobody likes lawyers—you should study business or something. Don't go to law school!" Suddenly, my original dream of becoming a jet-setting, cold-shower-taking entrepreneur felt much more urgent. As I began my second semester of law school, it seemed like I had to make a choice: either pursue my dream of becoming an entrepreneur or lead what Thoreau described as a life of "quiet desperation" in corporate law.[1]

Unfortunately, my parents, who had invested so much in my education, got a lot of social mileage out of my success as a student and didn't see it this way; they knew that Columbia Law—the fourth-ranked institution in the country according to U.S. News & World Report—is commonly referred to as the premier destination for landing a lucrative role at law firms around the world.[2][3] In fact, as I write this, the starting salary for a first-year associate at a large corporate law firm is $190,000, and 99 percent of Columbia Law graduates receive employment offers upon graduation.[4]

---

1 Henry David Thoreau, *Walden* (New York: Thomas Y. Crowell & Company, 1910), 8.

2 "2021 Best Law Schools," U.S. News & World Report, accessed October 21, 2020.

3 Karen Sloan, "Want to Work in Big Law? These Schools Are Good Bets," Law.com, published March 5, 2020.

4 "Employment Statistics," Columbia Law School, accessed August 28, 2020.

My parents knew that I seemed to enjoy law and that my current path would lead me to a high salary. Leaving all of that for a vague interest in "entrepreneurship" simply didn't make sense to them. However, I *knew* that if I didn't take a leave of absence from school to pursue my original dream, I would live with that regret for the rest of my life. So, with a few thousand dollars in the bank and a back-of-the-envelope plan in my pocket, I mustered all the confidence I could and jumped out of my debt-fueled plane to success.

I purposefully didn't tell my parents about my plan because I knew from experience that they'd be able to talk me out of it, especially since I hadn't fully thought things out and had no way to make money. For weeks, they thought I was still in school. When I finally told them what I'd done, they acted as if I had sucker-punched both of them in the gut, and my decision tested our relationship in ways I never could've imagined.

Leaving school was extremely painful for all of us despite my efforts to figure out ways to make it less painful. I talked to everyone I could and read every single blog or forum that addressed the question, "Should I go to/stay in law school?" Nothing helped.

So, I decided to write a book to solve this problem.

At its simplest, this book is designed to help two groups of people.

The first group consists of ambitious, hardworking students who are trying to decide whether to follow their passion or go with a more safe and secure career path.

The second group applies to those caring and involved parents, guardians, friends, and mentors who are trying to better understand the landscape that the student in their life faces and how to best support that student in having a happy, fulfilling, and *economically viable* life.

In this book, I will help guide both groups toward a better understanding of how to reconcile our natural inclination to explore our interests with the pragmatism that reality and survival oftentimes require.

I believe there is no better group to learn from than immigrants to accomplish this goal. Year after year, millions of well-meaning but often overbearing parents immigrate to the United States with the goal of bringing greater socioeconomic opportunity to their families. As such, many of these parents strongly encourage their children to enter professions that are highly regarded, highly paid, highly stable, or a combination of the three; the most commonly selected ones are doctor, lawyer, and engineer. While the parental motivations for desiring these careers varies, the impact is often the same: millions of kids who feel they must choose between living a life of their own that reflects their own interests and circumstances or receiving support, encouragement, and love from their parents.

In the following chapters, we'll explore the answers to the following questions:

- Why does the pressure to pursue these careers exist?
- Does the pressure to pursue these careers pay off in the ways that parents expect?

- What are the psychological and financial implications of this pressure?

We'll also hear stories from first- and second-generation Americans to examine the wide variety of ways that people have crafted their own American Dream. If you're a first-generation parent, this book will help you assist your child in living a more fulfilling and more successful life. If you're a child of said parent, this book will help you build a fulfilling life without bringing shame to your *entire* family.

And if you fall into neither of the aforementioned categories, you'll get more out of this book than anyone. You'll not only learn more about your first- and second-generation neighbors, but you'll also find that the stories are more similar to your life than different. At the end of the day, we all have to make similar decisions—whether to pursue the dream or take the stable career; whether to do what your parents want or follow your heart.

These are human stories. I look forward to you reading them.

1

YOU ARE HERE.

In Part One, we'll explore the backdrop of immigrant parenting styles and their effects on their children's interest development.

1

FOREIGN INVESTMENTS

With law school only a few weeks away, I found myself sitting in my parent's kitchen, preparing myself for the uproar that I would cause by sharing that I wanted to defer my entrance into law school. I knew this conversation would be stressful for me because, since childhood, I've been largely motivated by receiving approval and applause from my parents and other adults in positions of authority. There'd be no approval or applause here.

I also knew it would be stressful for my parents because throughout my life, they had gotten a lot of social mileage out of my near perfect track record and high educational performance. More importantly, however, they had invested nearly $200,000 of their own money into a prestigious ivy league education for me, and a deferral would mean their investment might go off the rails and all be for naught.

"I think I want to take some time off before law school to pursue my interests in entrepreneurship," I said sheepishly, bracing myself on the kitchen island that stood between me and my parents.

My mom's eyes grew wide. My dad contorted his face into his most disapproving scowl. This wasn't good.

My mom threw out the first parry. "I don't understand. It's been three years since you graduated from undergrad. You've taken the LSAT three times. You should just go and see. Maybe you'll like it."

She was right—it was confusing. I had spent three years working as a trademark paralegal at a large corporate law firm. I made great money, bought a condo, and from the outside at least, it looked like I enjoyed the work. I even had so much fun studying for the LSAT that I offered to be interviewed in a podcast about it.

But my mom hadn't seen me pitch my first start-up idea to a group of investors in college. She hadn't seen me source and organize a panel discussion on entrepreneurship. She hadn't seen me spend a year moonlighting with a small team to try and build an education tech start-up after work. All she saw was the beginning stages of my pet project called the University of Good (see: universityofgood.com), which at the time consisted of me spilling my guts on a podcast and posting my misadventures with binge eating and depression on Instagram. She had good reason to be concerned.

My dad also hadn't seen these things, but it likely wouldn't have mattered if he did. My dad was born in Nigeria and moved here when he was twenty-five to try and make a life in America. He had very little money and possessed what can only be described as *a lot* of hustle. After I was born, however, he realized he needed to be able to ensure that I always had a roof over my head and food to eat. So, he decided to become a nurse, which he knew would bring him a stable and substantial source of income. His friends would frequently tease him about being a male nurse, but my dad knew he could not allow their disapproval to stop him from doing what he felt he needed to do.

He worked extremely hard. To make ends meet when he first arrived in America, he worked as security guard at budget clothing store, Ross. After years of working eighty-hour weeks and completing two degree programs, he eventually worked his way up to chief nurse anesthetist at the prestigious Sibley Hospital in Washington, DC. As you can imagine, he expected high performances from me and my two younger siblings, but he also was willing to make sacrifices to help ensure that happened; I would later learn that he sold his first Mercedes Benz—a source of pride for him—so he could pay for my first year of college. He invested in me and my siblings with the hope that we would achieve even greater success and bring prestige to our family. In most cultures—especially those of immigrants—a degree from an Ivy League law school is a cause for celebration and is seen as a surefire ticket to success and bragging rights for years to come.

So, while I knew my dream of pursuing entrepreneurship hadn't disappeared, my parents had essentially exercised control through their disapproval, putting an end to my plan. Although they never explicitly said it, they knew their years of investment would go to waste if I messed up this opportunity. As I revoked my deferral and entered law school, I made a realization about my life: I'd had much less of a say on the direction in which it had unfolded than I'd thought.

* * *

My experience is common for many children of immigrants. Parents make a substantial investment in their kids, so they feel as though they have a controlling interest in the livelihood of said kids. Ironically enough, this experience is one that is also quite common in the field I was hoping to enter: entrepreneurship.

If you make a trip to any coffee shop in start-up hubs like Austin, Seattle, or San Francisco, one thing that you will definitely hear tossed around is the phrase "term sheet," meaning "a nonbinding agreement setting forth the basic terms and conditions under which an investment will be made."[5] Investors and start-up companies use them to lay out the initial conditions of their partnership following an investment from the investor. At its simplest, a term sheet should cover the high-level aspects of a deal without spelling out every minor detail and contingency that'll be covered in future contracts.[6]

According to Investopedia, a term sheet "essentially lays out the groundwork for ensuring that the parties involved in a business transaction agree on most major aspects of the deal, thereby precluding the possibility of a misunderstanding and lessening the likelihood of unnecessary disputes. It also ensures that expensive legal charges involved in drawing up a binding agreement or contract are not incurred prematurely."[7]

---

5 Investopedia, s.v. "Term Sheet," updated March 19, 2020.

6 Ibid.

7 Investopedia, s.v. "Term Sheet."

Term sheets make sense; if you're going make a sizable investment into an early-stage company—which is often times just an investment in an individual—you'll want to:

1. Make sure that you have some say over the future development of the company, and
2. Ensure that the company is successful so you can earn your expected return on your investment, if not more.

If you just checked the front cover to make sure you're still reading the same book, welcome back.

I'm giving you an Introduction to Economics lecture on term sheets because they share an uncanny resemblance to the way that many first-generation parents approach parenting. Their child is the budding start-up company and the parent is the eager angel investor—an individual who provides financial backing for small start-ups or entrepreneurs, typically in exchange for ownership equity in the company. Often, angel investors are found among an entrepreneur's family and friends. The funds that angel investors provide may be a one-time investment to help the business get off the ground or an ongoing contribution to carry the company through its difficult early stages.[8]

Not unlike angel investors, first-generation parents make large, ongoing monetary investments in their children that *still* pale in comparison to the sheer number of hours they spend raising them while adapting to a new culture. For many immigrant parents, these substantive investments

---

8 *Investopedia*, s.v. "Angel Investor," updated July 26, 2020.

are made solely for the sake of giving their children better economic opportunity and bringing prestige to their families.

In other words, in many first-generation families, a term sheet is ostensibly drawn up and signed before each child is born.

Although it is not a perfect analogy, many of the elements in a standard term sheet are also eerily similar to the implicit one that first-generation parents and their children figuratively sign upon birth:

1. **It's non-binding:** Neither the child nor the parent is obligated to abide by what's outlined on the term sheet in a court of law.
2. **Shared voting rights:** Children who receive extensive funding are usually at the mercy of their parents, who want to maximize the returns on their investment. This dynamic results in parents having disproportionate influence over determining the direction the child's life will take.
3. **Investor commitment:** How long will the parent wait before refusing to continue to invest in their child?[9]

If viewed through an investment angle, the parenting styles of first-generation immigrants make a lot of sense. The parents often have some money that they can invest, but not so much money that there's room to make a bad investment. Further, being new to the country, they tend to stick to industries that they are familiar with and have a proven record of providing a return on investment.

9 *Investopedia*, s.v. "Term Sheet."

Similarly, in certain start-up markets such as Seattle, the angel investors have a reputation of being risk averse; while there are certainly exceptions to the rule, many of the angel investors in Seattle are simply new to the investment world, and as such, to avoid making huge mistakes on their first endeavor, focus on companies with business models that they are relatively familiar with and *know* will virtually guarantee a return on investment.

Highly proven founder + a stellar team + a well-established market + a moderate improvement on an existing product or service = Seattle start-up slam dunk.

A stark contrast to Seattle is the behavior in a start-up ecosystem like Silicon Valley, where Yo, an app that only sends the word "Yo" between its users, raised $1.5 million in venture capital funding in less than a few months.[10] According to John China, president of Californian investment company SVB Capital, huge investments are common for Silicon Valley investors: "They tend to take more risk with angel portfolios and don't really track them or worry about them."[11]

As Silicon-Valley-based wealth advisor Miles Kruppa puts it, "People here are very comfortable with losing money on their investments...In San Francisco, this is a form of charity. It keeps the whole ecosystem working."[12]

---

10 Sarah Buhr, "Yo Raises $1.5M In Funding At A $10M Valuation, Investors Include Betaworks and Pete Cashmore," *TechCrunch*, published July 18, 2014.

11 Miles Kruppa, "For Silicon Valley Tech Tycoons, Angel Investing is a Status Symbol," *LA Times*, February 25, 2020.

12 Ibid.

If first-generation parents were compared to one of the aforementioned types of investors, it would certainly be the more risk-averse Seattleite. According to twenty years of research conducted by Tory Higgins, the director of the Motivation Science Center at Columbia University, first-generation immigrant parents may be risk-averse because they have what he terms a "prevention-focus." Higgins argues that people with a prevention-focus are not necessarily risk-averse because of anxiety, paranoia, or even a lack of self-confidence, but rather because they view goals as opportunities to maintain the status quo and keep things running smoothly. Those with this mindset usually have a deep aversion to wide-eyed optimism, mistake-making, and chance-taking.[13]

Thus, the goal for most Seattle investors and most first-generation parents—both of whom have an incentive to play it safe—isn't necessarily for their kid to hit a grand slam with the first swing; the real goal is for them to hit a solid double or triple and hope they can run to home base before their team strikes out.

To first-generation parents, hitting a double or triple means becoming a doctor, lawyer, or engineer. You will not necessarily be Babe Ruth, but the belief is that you will almost certainly make a six-figure salary, have a relatively stable job, and give your parents something to call home about.

Viewed from this lens, the behavior of immigrant parents makes quite a lot of sense. Their strategy is extremely

---

13 Heidi Grant, "The Hidden Danger of Being Risk-Averse," *Harvard Business Review*, July 2, 2013.

pragmatic and—at least from the outside—appears to be the best way to ensure they get a return on their investment.

But what do their children think about this strategy? They're the ones who carry out the parent's desired goal. So, the question becomes: is it pragmatic for the child to persevere through all circumstances and try to fulfill the terms of their "agreement"?

KEY TAKEAWAYS

- Your parents have made a substantial investment in you. Like any investor, they would like to see a return on their investment and would like some say in the direction of the venture.
- Your parents may be risk-averse, but it also may not be because they are overly paranoid; they may simply be prevention-focused and want to minimize mistakes.
- Their insistence on you becoming a doctor, lawyer, or engineer is likely because your parents believe such professions will a secure a return on their investment.

2

SURVIVAL

Extreme poverty. Gang banging. Killings. Stabbings. Drug dealers. Drug addicts. This was the environment of Haitian immigrant Pierre Laguerre, who moved to the United States in the early '90s with his mother and four siblings in search of a better life.

One could assume Laguerre lived through such terrible conditions in his poverty-stricken home nation of Haiti. However, he actually experienced them in his first neighborhood in the United States: Brooklyn, New York. Like many immigrants, Pierre was surprised to find out that America could look like this. Growing up in Haiti, Pierre's image of America was picturesque: bright beaches, tall towers, and a bevy of politicians, doctors, and lawyers striding to-and-fro.

This idyllic image of America heavily impacted Pierre, and he was clear about the path he would take to attain it.

> "Growing up in Haiti, I always wanted to become a neurologist. I was always amazed by the brain. Even as

> a kid, when I would do certain things to get a beating, I would ask myself: what is it that is causing me to do this? What is it that is causing me to behave this way when I just caught a beating for it the other day?"

As a young kid living in Haiti, where Pierre says, "it was evident you lived in a poor country," there was one singular goal: become a neurologist at Harvard Medical School

> "I wanted to become a doctor. In Haiti I knew Harvard University as one of the top universities to attend to get your law degree or medical degree, so in my mind, when I got to America, I knew what I was going to do."

Pierre's story thus far is reflective of many first-generation immigrants. America. Harvard. Doctor. For first-generation immigrants, these represent more than a country, a university, and a career; they're the American Dream.

However, when Pierre arrived in Brooklyn, NY, in the early '90s, the American Dream quickly became the American nightmare.

> "We weren't fortunate enough to live in a suburb, so we lived in Brooklyn at the time, and it was rough. Early 1990s Brooklyn was full of gangs, gang banging, and drug dealing. The streets were full of drug addicts.

> And in high school, kids were getting shot in school, stabbed in school—those kinds of things."

Pierre's plans to attend Harvard Medical School hung in the balance. Not because of a lack of interest in neurology, but rather because of a now more pressing interest: survival.

> "The dream of becoming a doctor went out of the window, and I started thinking about how I could escape."

The path to becoming a doctor, especially for a neurologist, is an extremely long road. Pierre would need four years of intensive undergraduate study, four years of expensive medical school, one year of interning, three years of a neurology residency, followed by up to *eight* (yes, you read that correctly) years of a neurology fellowship. That works out to a *minimum* of twelve years of schooling, all to have an average salary of $255,000 a year.[14]

While that's an impressive salary, with loan repayments, the opportunity cost of being in school instead of working, and the simple length of time required before earning that salary, it simply was not a feasible path for Pierre. His main priority was taking his family out of their dangerous environment.

---

14 "How to Become a Neurologist," American Academy of Neurology, accessed August 28, 2020.

While sitting in the living room of their Brooklyn apartment, Pierre told his mom that he no longer wanted to go to medical school and wanted to take a different route. Her response was not exactly supportive:

> "[Medical school] is what you are going to do. This is what we are as a people—we are Haitians. We are coming to America to become doctors, to become lawyers, and we take the opportunity that is provided to us to do something better for ourselves. . . you are going to graduate, you are going to become a doctor regardless of where we live now," Pierre recounted.

Pierre understood his mom's feelings and made a compromise by enrolling in community college to study electrical engineering. A four-year program would be substantially shorter than a twelve-year path to neurology and, as Pierre explained, would appease his mother who still very much wanted him to graduate and enter a prestigious profession.

But Pierre was one of four children, and with his single mom as the primary income earner, even putting himself through community college proved to be financially taxing for both him and his family. So, Pierre began looking for a faster way to make money, but he wasn't willing to rely on the crime and drug dealing that surrounded him to earn it.

"I studied the statistics, and said, 'I don't want that. I don't want to become a product of that environment. How do I go about getting out of here?'"

The answer for Pierre came in the form of truck driving. According to the Bureau of Labor Statistics May 2019 report, a truck drivers average salary is $45,260 a year, with the top 10 percent making roughly $66,840.[15] After a few months of training, you're on the road and making a decent salary.[16] At the very least, it would solve Pierre's money issues and satisfy his intellectual curiosity.

"I got to travel the country... make some money, explore America, and take care of my mom and my siblings."

Making this decision certainly didn't come easily. Pierre thoroughly considered the implications that trucking would have on his family.

> "Coming from the Caribbean, we also grow up with the expectation that if we're here [in the US], we've been granted this opportunity to be here at such an early age. . . now it's our job—our duty—to build something so we can send something back home. It's not just your mom. . . you still have other family back home who are depending on you. . . it comes with a lot of pressure. So, when you say, 'I'm not going to become a doctor, I am going to go drive a truck,' in their eyes you pretty much just killed their whole dream. They were counting on that doctor money. You killed everyone's dream."

---

15 "Occupational Employment and Wages, May 2019, 53-3032 Heavy and Tractor-Trailer Truck Drivers," U.S. Bureau of Labor Statistics, last modified July 6, 2020.

16 "Becoming a CDL Driver," CDL.com, accessed August 28, 2020.

I remember the day when I first threatened to kill my family's dream. It was two weeks before I was to begin at Columbia Law School. Everyone was excited and enthused. My dad had already started researching whether or not Columbia Law sweaters came in his size. I had done it; in three years, I would hold two degrees—both from Ivy league institutions—and would be an esteemed member of the legal profession.

I, on the other hand, was distraught. For a multitude of reasons, my summer before law school had absolutely destroyed my passion for the law. In a sudden turn of events, the idea of becoming a lawyer had turned from a source of pride into a source of shame.

That summer, I had been accepted into a prestigious fellowship program for minority law students. As part of the fellowship, I was assigned a summer associate position at an emerging boutique law firm in Washington, DC. The firm treated me well; they took me out for expensive meals and involved me in high-profile cases. I even casually met Barack Obama while taking the elevator in the building that we shared. Despite these experiences, I would return home every day and look through my window at all the seemingly happy people who, at least from the outside looking in, appeared to have successfully managed to pursue their own dreams, turn hobbies into careers, start companies, or backpack through Asia. And there I was, planning to go to law school, only to work insanely long hours, navigate firm politics, and participate in a perpetual rat race with other lawyers to make more money than any of us actually need.

This view was of course skewed, and in time I would come to realize exactly how much I enjoyed legal practice. But that was not the case that summer before law school, and I decided I wanted to take some time off before starting. I just wanted two years to follow my entrepreneurship dream. But when I told my parents about this idea of mine, they didn't exactly receive it with the same excitement as they did when I told them about my plans to go to law school.

Pierre found himself in a similar situation, with the additional shame of leaving college to become a truck driver. He recalled when he first dropped out of school, he tried to avoid being seen out of embarrassment.

With time and continued work, Pierre grew more secure in his decision:

> "It's not about what everyone else dreams. It's also about what I dream for myself. If I'm worried about achieving dreams for everyone else, then guess what—I am a dreamer, not a do-er."

> "Once I started looking at things in that sense, I was kind of like, 'I couldn't give two Fs what your dream was for me. Because your dream does not dictate my current circumstances.'"

> "Because you could go eight years and still not actually become a doctor. What happens to the students who fail their exams and have to switch to another career? We have to talk about them, too. You can do all of that just to appease someone, and then fail your

exams. That's when people feel like a failure. Then we start feeling like life isn't fair, like we aren't capable of achieving anything because we had this weight on our shoulders to do this particular thing. You might realize you weren't really good at it, and you might have genuinely been better off as a truck driver."

Pierre's point can be backed up by data:

> "In recent years, about six percent of U.S. medical school graduates have not moved into residencies each year," says Kevin Lynn, founder of Doctors without Jobs. "If you don't get a residency, you cannot be licensed to practice as a doctor. We cannot continue to ask our best and brightest to commit four years of their lives to higher education and another four years to specialized education in medicine – taking on hundreds of thousands of dollars in student debt and then say, 'Sorry, you can't work as a doctor.'"[17]

If you end up being one of the students who fall into this category, your degree can suddenly become an albatross and your dream of becoming a doctor much less certain.

Armed with his new perspective, Pierre felt certain about his path. He was a truck driver even though his mother's dream of him bringing renown to the family appeared to be on its last legs.

---

17 PRNewswire, "Doctors without Jobs Says Recent Residency Match Leaves More U.S. Physicians Jobless," Business Insider, published April 22, 2019.

After trucking for a few years, however, something interesting happened. The intellectually curious Pierre saw an opportunity to turn his truck driving into a trucking business. His mother, however—a former entrepreneur in her own right as a seamstress in Haiti—was not a fan of this idea at all.

"And so I said, 'Ma, I'm thinking I might start my own business.' And she did not want to hear that," Pierre recalled.

As you remember, Pierre's mother, like many first-generation immigrant parents, was adamant about him becoming a doctor, lawyer, or engineer. In her mind, this trucking thing was a temporary stop before Pierre came to his senses and decided to return to school. Yet Pierre had made a realization while following his own path as a truck driver. Driving miles and miles across the country, Pierre met hundreds of Americans. He saw in vivid technicolor that although the country was not necessarily gold-paved streets filled with doctors, lawyers, and politicians, there were a plethora of other paths to genuinely succeed in America.

Paths that did not require him being a doctor, lawyer, or engineer.

Paths that did not require a dozen years of education and several hundred thousands of dollars in debt.

Pierre recounted the moment he explained this to his mom in their small apartment in Brooklyn:

> "I said to her, 'Mama this country not only provides you with the opportunity to become a doctor or to

> become a lawyer.' My argument was that every wealthy person in this country became wealthy because they learned one thing. They learned how to start a business; they learned how to buy their time back."

Despite his mother's resistance, Pierre persisted. Over the course of ten years, he started two multi-million-dollar trucking companies and founded a venture-backed start-up aimed at connecting truck drivers to trucking jobs.

He had done it.

Despite the familial pressure and his own self-doubt, he managed to achieve his own American Dream of starting a company and moving his family out of poverty. But as he explained, Pierre was a natural born rebel. He was accustomed to doing things his own way. However, many children feel that they have no choice but to do what their parents believe is the best option. Let's figure out why.

KEY TAKEAWAYS

- It's possible that your dream won't be everything that you predicted it to be.
- If you see an opportunity that your parents don't see because of your differences in perspective, don't ignore it just because your parents said so.
- Going to medical school is not a guarantee for security and it's possible to achieve success in America without becoming a doctor, lawyer, or engineer.

3

MOTHERS OF TIGERS

Parenting is a hard job. Sure, there are books on how to be a better parent, but for several reasons, it is still very, very hard.

The hours are long and unpredictable.

Your clients—kids—are emotionally unstable, entitled, and also happen to be your roommates.

Plus, the world often looks down on your parenting decisions.

According to sociologist Paul Verhaeghe, on top of their own duty to succeed, parents are frequently held responsible for the successes and failures of their children. "Should a young person be unable to navigate an increasingly competitive social milieu, then it is not just their failure, it is also the parents' failure too."[18] This internalized concern for one's child's success is called child-contingent self-esteem. This

18 Thomas Curran and Andrew P. Hill, "Perfectionism Is Increasing over Time: A Meta-Analysis of Birth Cohort Differences from 1989 to 2016," *American Psychological Association - Psychological Bulletin 145, no. 4,* (2019): 410-429.

phenomenon has risen alongside parental expectations for their children's achievements which—across the industrialized world—are so extreme that psychologists are concerned.[19]

So, while one may love their kids, parenting is still certainly not a job for the faint of heart. Today, there is a new complication that, for some, has transformed parenting into the single most difficult job in the world: the notion of a "successful" parent is extremely difficult to define. To explain why, let's go back several thousand years to the Mesozoic era.

As cavemen and cavewomen, "successful" parenting was hard, but simple: Keep. Child. Alive.

As we handled basic survival needs, our attention then focused to other human interests such as the desire for love and belonging, self-esteem, self-actualization, and even transcendence. American psychologist Abraham Maslow explained this phenomenon in his widely popular theory known as "Maslow's Hierarchy of Needs."[20]

Maslow's Hierarchy of Needs is an extremely widespread motivational theory in psychology that comprises of a five-tier model of human needs, often depicted as hierarchical levels within a pyramid. Maslow's theory argues that needs lower in the hierarchy must be satisfied before individuals can attend to higher needs. From the bottom up, the hierarchy of needs consists of physiological, safety, love and

19 Ibid.

20 Saul McLeod, "Maslow's Hierarchy of Needs," SimplyPsychology, last updated March 20, 2020.

belonging, esteem, and self-actualization.[21] Our cave moms and cave dads sat at the bottom of this pyramid, seeking simply to provide their children with physiological needs like food, water, and basic shelter. As they learned how to satisfy those needs, they progressed up the pyramid, and the question of how to provide for their children naturally became less simple to define.

For example, take the second level of the hierarchy, safety and security: "Safety and security needs are about keeping us safe from harm. These include shelter, job security, health, and safe environments. If a person does not *feel* safe in an environment, they will seek to find safety before they attempt to meet any higher level of survival."[22] Although still rather basic, it's clear that at this level, we've moved from pure physiological needs to the needs of the heart and spirit. It's not just about being physically safe; it's also about *feeling* safe. For a parent, the task of ensuring that their child *feels* safe is much less clear-cut than making sure your child has food to eat and water to drink.

As we continue up the hierarchy to social belonging, self-esteem, self-actualization, and transcendence, the answers become even more vague.

How important are a child's friendships to her overall life satisfaction?

Should I plan play dates? If so, how many?

---

21 McLeod, "Maslow's Hierarchy of Needs."

22 James Kelly, "Maslow's Hierarchy of Needs," The Peak Performance Center, accessed October 8, 2020.

What if someone bullies my kid on a play date? How can I protect her self-esteem? Should I?

Perhaps I should sit back and watch from the sidelines so that she can fight her own battles and become self-actualized—a fancy psychological term for when one achieves their highest potential.[23]

Or maybe I'm over-stressing this. Maybe this hierarchy of needs is a farce. Maybe after health and safety, it's nothing more than a hierarchy of *nice-to-haves.*

These are the questions that many of today's parents have to grapple with.

But in some cultures, there's no grappling.

The question is quite simple:

Doctor, lawyer, or engineer?

This is the only hierarchy.

Yale Law School professor Amy Chua coined "tiger mother" in her 2011 memoir *Battle Hymn of the Tiger Mother.* The term refers to a parenting style that is primarily attributed to Asian families, and one that minimizes individualism, encourages discipline, and produces extremely high levels of academic achievement.[24]

---

23 *Merriam-Webster,* s.v. "self-actualize (v.)," accessed September 4, 2020.

24 Su Yeong Kim, "Defining Tiger Parenting in Chinese Americans," Human Development 56, no. 4 (September 2013): 217–222.

"Chinese parents can do things that would seem unimaginable -- even legally actionable -- to Westerners. Chinese mothers can say to their daughters, 'Hey fatty -- lose some weight.' By contrast, Western parents have to tiptoe around the issue, talking in terms of 'health' and never ever mentioning the f-word, and their kids still end up in therapy for eating disorders and negative self-image. ... Western parents are concerned about their children's psyches. Chinese parents aren't. They assume strength, not fragility, and as a result they behave very differently."[25]

EXCERPT FROM BATTLE HYMN OF THE TIGER MOTHER

According to Dr. Cha-Hsuan Liu, a university lecturer at the Department of Interdisciplinary Social Science at Utrecht University and a proud, self-proclaimed "tiger mom," there's nothing inherently wrong with this parenting style.[26]

In Dr. Liu's TEDx talk from 2018, she explains the reason behind tiger parenting through an old Chinese parable of a woman who traveled to three different countries, searching "for the best educational opportunities for her son's education and growth."[27]

---

25 Amy Chua, Battle Hymn of The Tiger Mother (New York: The Penguin Press, 2010), 87–88.

26 Cha-Hsuan Liu, TEDx Talks, "The Secret of Tiger Moms," published June 14, 2017, YouTube Video, 13:35.

27 Cha-Hsuan Liu, TEDx Talks, "The Secret of Tiger Moms," published June 14, 2017, YouTube Video, 13:35.

According to Dr. Liu, Chinese parents have followed the path of this woman for centuries, doing the same thing. Why? "Because education is the foundation for a child's development and his or her possibility in a society."[28]

While research appears to support this assumption, most everyday parents also would agree with such an assertion.[29] It's one of the main reasons why Americans are in greater student loan debt than ever before.

Dr. Liu states that although we all clearly care about our children's education, the question of "how to do it, differs between the east and the west."[30] Dr. Liu received her education from both worlds; she completed her early education and master's degrees in China and Taiwan and earned her PhD from the Netherlands.

"When meeting people from the west for the first time, I am often confronted with this question: 'Heyyyy,'" Dr. Liu uttered in her best Dutch accent, stretching out each of her vowels. "'I heard about Asian parenting styles... Are you a tiger mom?'"[31]

Dr. Liu's reenactment of this scene portrays the inquisitive westerners as being fearful that her answer might be yes. As noted by the excerpt from Chua's memoir, for many western parents, the parenting style of tiger moms is cruel and limits

---

28 Liu, "The Secret of Tiger Moms."

29 Stacy Dale and Alan B. Krueger, "Estimating the Return to College Selectivity over the Career Using Administrative Earnings Data," Journal of Human Resources 49, no. 2 (Spring 2014): 323-358.

30 Liu, "The Secret of Tiger Moms."

31 Ibid.

their child's individuality. However, for Dr. Liu, this is far from a concern.

"I am a Mom, and I care about my son's education. And I am well-prepared, physically and mentally, to fight for the constraints that exist in our environment to ensure the best education for my son."[32]

According to Dr. Liu, there is a common set of beliefs—a set of "secrets"—shared among all tiger mothers. These secrets are what Dr. Liu believes allow Asian children to perform higher than their peers in almost any society and in almost any country.[33]

BELIEF 1: EDUCATION LEADS TO POSITIVE SOCIAL MOVEMENT

> "My family moved from Malin, China, to Wuhan after the second world war," remarked Dr. Liu. "Throughout my education and childhood, my family constantly reminded me, 'You need to work hard because education is the only way to move us from the current social class to a wealthier living.' The whole family worked together to ensure that the best education could be received by our next generation. And the teachers and the schools are expected to work together to bring out the best development for the child."[34]

32 Ibid.

33 Ibid.

34 Liu, "The Secret of Tiger Moms."

In China, teachers are revered and have a special role in society. Every year since the middle ages, China celebrates "Teachers Day" on September 10, Confucius' birthday.[35] Confucius was China's most famous teacher, philosopher, and political theorist, and his ideas have been extremely influential in the development of East Asia.[36]

The decision to celebrate teachers on the day of Confucius' birth speaks to something important about education and the tiger mom parenting style: from the perspective of a "tiger mom," pushing your child toward educational excellence isn't necessarily seen as being overbearing or insensitive to a child's needs. Instead, it's simply a part of a centuries-long belief that education is paramount to success.

BELIEF 2: EVERY CHILD HAS TALENTS

The second tenet of the tiger mom belief system is that all children have talents to be cultivated, and making that happen is a shared responsibility between the teachers and the parents.

As such, it'll come to no surprise that many tiger parents will assign their kids to a wide variety of activities and subjects to tease out those talents:

Mathematics.

---

35 "Teacher's Day - Festive Date in China," Advantour, accessed September 5, 2020.

36 Encyclopaedia Britannica Online, Academic ed., s.v. "Confucius," accessed September 5, 2020.

Literature.
Dance.
Music.
Piano.
Arts.

"Now you know why Asian kids do not have time to play with other kids after school," remarked Dr. Liu with a lighthearted smile. Although she was joking, there's a lot of truth to her statement. "When I was in high school, the school started at 7:30 in the morning. Ended at 5:00. Sometimes we stayed at school until 7:00 or 9:00 p.m. If there's important exams ahead, we were expected to go to school on the weekends."[37]

According to Dr. Liu, her parents would always say, "You will be somebody in the future," and typically compared her to neighboring children or her cousins and relatives.[38]

- "Hey come on, the neighbor's kid got a ninety-nine for his grade so you can do it."
- "Your cousin won the first prize at a piano contest, so you can do it, too."

In the west, parents may meet this manner of thinking with Theodore Roosevelt's famous quote, "Comparison is the thief of joy." Perhaps comparison is the thief of joy, but it may also be a generous provider of motivation and drive to achieve academic excellence and earn a handsome income.

---

37 Liu, "The Secret of Tiger Moms."

38 Ibid.

According to social psychologists Adam Galinsky and Maurice Schweitzer, social comparison is an innate human tendency and—whether it's the wisest move or not—it's a big part of the way we determine our own level of happiness and motivation. To prove this point, Galinsky and Schweitzer reference a classic study by Emory University scientist Frans de Waal.[39]

> "De Waal trained capuchin monkeys to essentially use stones as a kind of currency, exchanging one for a nice cucumber slice. The monkeys were perfectly happy with this arrangement, until de Waal started giving some, but not all, of the monkeys a sweet, juicy grape instead of the cucumber. (Like humans, monkeys would much rather have something sweet than a boring vegetable.)
>
> Upon seeing this inequity, the monkey who was offered the regular cucumber went, well, apeshit," Galinsky and Schweitzer write. The monkeys who perceived themselves as receiving a lesser deal became visibly upset, refusing to pay for the cucumber or sometimes even throwing the slice back in the experimenter's face. "What this experiment demonstrates," the authors write, "is that our evolutionary ancestors did not evaluate their outcomes in isolation; rather, they evaluated outcomes in a comparative process."[40]

---

39 Melissa Dahl, "Comparison is the thief of joy, so why can't we stop?," CNN Health, accessed September 5, 2020.

40 Ibid.

Dr. Liu shared how this comparative nature played out in her school environment. "In school, my teacher gave us individual goals for [an assignment], and then paired us with each other, who are from the same level, in order to compete. After we received the results, I received a ninety, and my competitor got eighty-eight. My competitor would get punishment for two points lost. I was the winner, but I didn't reach my goal, which was ninety-five, so my teacher would punish me by beating me on my hands with a stick."[41]

According to Dr. Liu, this emphasis on high marks is not about how much you have learned, but simply about the scores themselves:

"Grades for any Asian student are not an indicator for how much you have learned, or how much you have achieved, but a reference to tell you where you stand at this moment, and where you are expected to go further."[42]

Certainly, one learns a lot through such an intensive study process. However, as Dr. Liu says, the learning is not the emphasis—the scores, not unlike in a video game, are what's important.

Educational purists may scoff at this idea, but reality shows that scores are often the most important metric when it comes to earning more money. For example, law schools typically give out scholarships based on GPA and LSAT

41 Cha-Hsuan Liu, "The Secret of Tiger Moms."

42 Ibid.

scores.[43] Many law firms hire and give out bonuses based on law school grades and billable hours.[44] Scholarship organizations and jobs typically filter by college and high school GPA.[45]

For someone primarily interested in the earning boost associated with education, optimizing for higher scores isn't a bad approach.[46]

BELIEF 3: HARD WORK BEATS TALENT

Dr. Liu argues that many parents in the west claim that their child is simply not talented enough to achieve these high scores, no matter how much they are pushed.[47]

She also has an answer for such parents: "Hard work beats talent."[48]

Ironically, this is an idea that most western families can get behind. Thomas Edison once said, "genius is one percent inspiration and ninety-nine percent perspiration."[49] The idea

---

43 "LSAT Scores: The Good, The Bad & The Average," Chegg, accessed September 5, 2020.

44 *Vault Guide to the Top 100 Law Firms, 2018 Edition*, s.v. "Cooley LLP," Vault, accessed October 8, 2020.

45 Marissa, "Why Your GPA Matters," *College Dreams* (blog), *The California State University*, accessed October 8, 2020.

46 Eduardo Porter, "A Simple Equation: More Education = More Income," *New York Times*, published September 10, 2014.

47 Liu, "The Secret of Tiger Moms."

48 Ibid.

49 "ForbesQuotes: Thoughts on the Business of Life" Forbes, accessed September 5, 2020.

here is that if you can get your kids to work hard enough, it's not that important how much inherent talent they have.

"Asian students' high performance in the world cannot be explained by their individual talents, but by practice, and practice, and practice, again and again, under the supervision of their tiger mothers," Dr. Liu remarked proudly. *"Opportunities are for those who are prepared. . .Tiger moms want to prepare their children before the opportunity arises."*[50]

The three beliefs of tiger mothers make sense from a parenting standpoint, but what about the child in the situation? While they may rank high in their class, where do they rank on Maslow's hierarchy of needs? Dr. Liu understands and acknowledges this issue of the tiger mother approach. "No matter how strict the tiger moms, no matter busy they are preparing their children, Asian parents nowadays have started to be aware of the happiness we may take away from our children."[51]

Dr. Liu points out that new tiger moms are still holding the three beliefs but also consider strategies from the west. She believes that by synthesizing the approaches, we may be able to design an idyllic educational system for our children. "It is my dream and mission for my son and for our children to have a stimulating and instructive education system where there is freedom to discover the world and self, and where there is discipline to reach their goals."[52]

---

50 Liu, "The Secret of Tiger Moms."

51 Ibid.

52 Ibid.

Sounds like a fair deal to me, but the truth is, the implementation of such an idealized educational system waits far away in the future. For now, let's explore the psychological impacts of tiger parenting on children.

4

PARENTING, PERFECTIONISM, AND PSYCHOPATHOLOGY

I grew up in a household familiar to many other children of immigrants, with an unambiguous expectation of good grades and subtle scorn at anything less than perfect scores. Discipline and the smell of some kind of stew or rice filled the air, regardless of the occasion. Yelling was the primary form of communication. Errors and mistakes such as leaving a cabinet open could be met with a fury like never seen before. And although this may all seem like a bad childhood to those who did not grow up in such in an environment, many of us look back with fondness and laugh at the sheer insanity of our years growing up with our parents.

As you can imagine, this manner of parenting does come with positive consequences such as high performance in academics; Nigerian immigrants and their children are one of the most educated groups in the United States.

> "Although they make up a tiny portion of the U.S. population, in 2006, a whopping thirty-seven percent of all Nigerians in the United States held a bachelor's degree, seventeen percent had a master's degree, and four percent held a doctorate, according to the American Community Survey conducted by the U.S. Census Bureau. To put those numbers in perspective, only roughly nineteen percent of white residents had bachelor's degrees, eight percent had master's degrees, and one percent held doctorates in 2006, according to the Census survey. Asian Americans come closer to Nigerians with twelve percent holding master's degrees and three percent having doctorates."[53]

Another consequence of this manner of parenting, however, is that it frequently results in the cultivation of unhealthy perfectionism within the children. In psychology, perfectionism is a personality style characterized by a person's concern with striving for flawlessness and perfection and, in its unhealthier forms, is accompanied by overly critical self-evaluations and deep concern regarding others' evaluations.[54] In another way, while "healthy" perfectionists derive pleasure from accomplishing difficult tasks, "unhealthy" perfectionists never feel that what they have done is good enough.

---

53 Leslie Casimir, "Data Show Nigerians the Most Educated in the U.S.," *Houston Chronicle*, last modified January 12, 2018.

54 Joachim Stoeber and Julian H. Childs, "The Assessment of Self-Oriented and Socially Prescribed Perfectionism: Subscales Make a Difference," *Journal of Personality Assessment* 92, no. 6 (2010): 577–585.

[55]According to Dr. Mary Odafe, a researcher at the University of Houston and author of the 2020 study, "Maladaptive Perfectionism, Expressive Suppression, and Familism Among Young Adult Children of Immigrants: Risk or Resilience to Suicide Ideation?," this unhealthy perfectionism is particularly common in children of immigrants:

> "Many first- and second-generation American young adults share similar cultural experiences—growing up in a household with lofty expectations for achievement. Still, there is an intrinsic desire to honor our parents who sacrificed so much to build a life for us. Interestingly, ethnic minority individuals across this generational group consistently show greater psychological vulnerability than their foreign-born parents."[56]

Substantive psychological research shows that "the immediate family environment, and parental practices in particular, shape the development of perfectionism at an individual level."[57] In my family, the pressure on me and my siblings to be perfect was a near constant. A dish left out after dinner could lead to a long, loud scolding. Grades below an "A" were reason for serious discussions at the dinner table. Of course, high performance would be met with rewards like money and special food items like pound cake, my favorite.

---

55 Gordon Flett et al., *Perfectionism: Theory, Research, and Treatment*, (Washington, DC: American Psychological Association, 2002), 89–132.

56 Ike Evans, "Children of Immigrants: Psychological Risk and Resilience," Hogg Foundation for Mental Health, University of Texas, September 17, 2019.

57 Gordon Flett et al., *Perfectionism: Theory, Research, and Treatment*, (Washington, DC: American Psychological Association, 2002), 89–132.

Thus, the drive to be perfect came not only from a fear of punishment but also from a desire to receive approval and rewards from our parents.

Psychologist Jim Taylor calls this type of parenting "outcome love," and argues that it can be communicated either openly or subtly to children.

> "Some parents become so invested in their children's achievements, whether academic, athletic, or artistic, that they actively reward success and punish failure. These parents reward success by giving their love in the form of effusive praise, physical affection, and lavish gifts. When these parents perceive that their children have failed, they punish their children with expressions of disappointment, anger, and derision, or by withholding love with neglect, emotional distance, absence of physical contact, and withdrawal of support and encouragement."[58]

Taylor argues that this approach to parenting is misguided. He posits that while the children will achieve some degree of success with this approach, they will likely never fully realize their ability, as they are being driven by fear. Further, Taylor notes that because of the relentless pressure to succeed, the children are more likely to miss the values and behaviors (e.g., hard work, honesty, discipline, etc.) that allow them to be happy and productive members of society in the long haul.[59]

---

58 Jim Taylor, "Parenting: Conditional Love is Good!", *Psychology Today*, published January 7, 2010.

59 Ibid.

Taylor believes parents should use what he calls "value love," in which parental love is conditional on children adopting essential values and acting in socially appropriate and ethical ways.

> "Value love nurtures the development of positive values and moral behavior, fosters healthy growth, and encourages achievement and happiness. You can instill values and life skills, such as respect, responsibility, hard work, discipline, compassion, and generosity, by giving praise-offering love when your children demonstrate these values and showing disapproval-withholding love when your children don't demonstrate these values," says Taylor.[60]

By employing "value love," Taylor believes that parents will still reach their ultimate goal of having their child be successful because it instills values and life skills such as hard work and discipline, while also allowing the child to be happy, fulfilled, and a good person.[61]

One may retort that in the case of immigrant parents, the goal is not for the child to be "fully realized" or to be "happy"; the goal is simply for the child to be *partially* realized, but ***fully*** stable and economically secure. However, according to Taylor, "outcome love" can get in the way of that goal as well.

> "With outcome love, children sense that their parents are acting on their own needs and interests rather than on what is best for their children. This perception

60 Ibid.

61 Taylor, "Parenting: Conditional Love."

> can create several harmful results. It causes conflict between children and parents that can generate anger, resentment, and resistance on the part of the children. Parents, in turn, likely unaware of their use of this bad form of conditional love, are bitter toward their children whom they perceive to be ungrateful for their parents' efforts to help them succeed. The ultimate result of this conflict is that children may act against their own best interests by sabotaging their efforts to exact revenge on their parents. And, sadly, the relationship between parent and child is severely damaged, sometimes irreparably."[62]

Despite Dr. Taylor's wishes, in reality, most immigrant parents (and parents in general) don't actually parent with "value love." As such, most children of immigrant parents have some—read: a lot of—perfectionist traits. The question is, what do those traits mean for these children and their future career plans? The available research has some answers.

As alluded to earlier, one way that researchers have conceptualized perfectionism is by thinking of it as two separate yet overlapping factors. The first factor is "perfectionistic strivings," most commonly associated with self-oriented perfectionism—one's personal need for perfection. The second factor is "perfectionistic concerns," commonly associated with being overly self-critical of mistakes, believing that others impose one's need for perfection, and reacting negatively to imperfection.[63]

---

62 Ibid.

63 *Oxford Research Encyclopedia, Psychology*, s.v. "Perfectionism and Performance in Sport, Education, and the Workplace," accessed October 8,

As you can imagine, children of immigrants frequently express more of the "perfectionistic concerns," since their childhood experiences taught them to worry about mistakes. They also believe that others—their parents, for example—impose the need for perfection and as such have very negative reactions to imperfection.

As a result, many children of immigrants, in hopes of being the "perfect child," decide to enter one of the "approved" professions like law, medicine, or engineering. However, this behavior isn't useful in the long run; research shows that perfectionistic concerns "show almost exclusively positive relationships with maladaptive outcomes (e.g., burnout) and negative relationships with adaptive outcomes (e.g., self-esteem)."[64]

Burnout is a state of emotional, mental, and often physical exhaustion from prolonged or repeated stress.[65] It's not an official medical diagnosis, but Paula Davis-Laack, who holds a master's degree in positive psychology and frequently works with lawyers, defines burnout as "a disease of disengagement."[66]

The core symptoms of people who experience burnout are:

- **Fatigue, no matter how much someone rests or sleeps.** This is an exhaustion that runs deeper than sleep deprivation, and it can't be cured by a few days off.

2020.

64 Ibid.

65 "Burnout," *Psychology Today*, accessed September 11, 2020.

66 Kate Mangan, "How to Recognize and Prevent Lawyer Burnout," Lawyerist, last modified August 1, 2019.

- **Cynicism about life and feeling like nothing they do really matters.** They feel a lack of excitement about their work and major successes they once strove for and feel generally disengaged.
- **A sense of inefficacy.** They're exerting significant effort but aren't making any progress or gaining any recognition.
- **Lack of attention.** Inability to focus is a key symptom of burnout, says Davis-Laack.[67]

These symptoms frequently cause people to leave their "prestigious" and "stable" jobs, and many leave in a poor mental state from which they never recover. In fact, one-third of the reason for physician turnover in healthcare can be attributed to burnout.[68] Almost forty percent of IT managers report burnout as their biggest concern for their engineers.[69] Law is the only profession with an entire industry made up of companies that are devoted to helping current members quit (side note: for any lawyers reading, I can personally vouch that the best one is formerlawyer.com started by UChicago grad Sarah Cottrell).[70]

These professions are stressful enough in themselves, but compounded with unhealthy perfectionism and the added stress that comes with being an underrepresented minority, burnout is substantially more likely.[71] Immigrant parents

---

67 Ibid.

68 Paula Davis-Laack, "I Fought the Law And the Law Won: My Burnout Story," *Forbes*, published May 17, 2018.

69 Sam Lewis, "Why VPs Should Care About Engineer Burnout," *PagerDuty Blog*, PagerDuty, published September 8, 2015.

70 Mangan, "How to Recognize and Prevent Lawyer Burnout."

71 Emma Wadsworth et al., "Racial Discrimination, Ethnicity and Work Stress," *Occupational Medicine* 57, no. 1 (2007): 18–24.

expect academic excellence so their children can become doctors, lawyers, or engineers; however, it will all be for naught if said child burns out.

In light of these statistics, when deciding whether to pursue your dream career or to stick with the tried and true, pay close attention to what you'd want from each potential path. Is it to fulfill a personal interest of yours? Is it because you feel you need the money? Or is it because you believe doing so is a way to avoid making a mistake? Law, medicine, and engineering can make for truly fulfilling and lucrative careers. However, if your reason for pursuing them centers around wanting to be perfect and believing that imperfection would threaten your self-worth or your parents' love, you should pause and reconsider whether it's actually the right move.

In part three of this book, we'll discuss exactly how to sort out the "right" path for you, but first we'll discover why we have these paths to choose from in the first place.

KEY TAKEAWAYS

- Immigrant parenting styles frequently lead to high performance, but they can also lead to what is known as "unhealthy perfectionism."
- Unhealthy perfectionism is marked by a fear of not being perfect, as opposed to striving for perfection, and can lead to low performance and burnout.
- Careers in law, medicine, and engineering can be fruitful, stable, and fulfilling, but it's harder to reap these benefits if the fear of not being perfect is your motivating factor.

5

DEVELOPING YOUR INTERESTS

As previously discussed, the primary metric of success for children of immigrants is often simply whether or not our parents are pleased with our behavior. We're reared from an early age to put emphasis on good grades, long hours of studying, and as many accolades as we can acquire. Our parents often don't encourage our interests unless such interests might lead to "success."

Considering this dynamic, although many children of immigrants have a nagging feeling that being a doctor, lawyer, or engineer is not right for them, their interests were so neglected that many are unable to even consider what else they would do. In this chapter we'll explore why this happens and what some potential remedies could be.

Social Cognitive Career Theory (SCCT), a psychological model developed by Robert W. Lent, Steven D. Brown, and Gail Hackett in 1994, explains how basic academic and career interests develop and offers a promising explanation for the lack of awareness of one's own interests. According to the model, there are three intrinsically linked variables that serve as the basic building blocks for any individual analysis of how basic academic and career interests are developed.[72] We'll discuss the two relevant ones here.

VARIABLE 1: SELF-EFFICACY

> "Self-efficacy refers to an individual's personal beliefs about his or her capabilities to perform particular behaviors or courses of action. For example, one person might feel very confident in being able to accomplish tasks for successful entry into, and performance in, scientific fields but feel much less confident about his or her abilities in social or enterprising fields, such as sales."[73]

The basic assumption behind SCCT is that people are more likely to become interested in, choose to pursue, and perform better in activities in which they have strong self-efficacy beliefs, as long as they also have necessary skills and environmental supports to pursue these activities.[74]

This variable actually explains why I wrote this book; my self-efficacy beliefs for becoming a published author are extremely high. I love reading and writing, and I've published

72 "Social Cognitive Career Theory," Career Research, accessed September 14, 2020.

73 Ibid.

74 Ibid.

multiple pieces of writing since eighth grade. Additionally, I have the necessary skills (i.e., I wrote well enough to get into a top five law school), and my current environment (i.e., an online book writing program with dozens of other authors) is extremely conducive to the pursuit. As the self-efficacy variable suggests, I had a substantive interest in writing a book, I chose to pursue it, and as far as I can tell, I'm performing better at it than I would at trying to become a theoretical physicist, for example.

That said, as Othanya Garcia, a Columbia University graduate and student at New York Medical College, points out, self-efficacy beliefs are malleable, and you should not allow them to limit your dreams. "If your reason to quit pursuing your dream is because you feel like you can't do it, then you need to stop that way of thinking. You need to find resources that can help you." Othanya initially had substantial doubts about her ability to get into medical school after struggling with her pre-med courses in undergrad. She had serious thoughts about giving up altogether, but after surrounding herself with helpful support systems and learning more about her unique skillsets by working with a career counselor, she was able to increase her self-efficacy beliefs, push through adversity, and successfully achieve her goal.

VARIABLE 2: OUTCOME EXPECTATIONS

> Outcome expectations refer to "beliefs about the consequences or outcomes of performing particular behaviors (e.g., what will happen if I do this?). The choices that people make about the activities in which

they will engage, and their effort and persistence at these activities, entail consideration of outcome as well as self-efficacy beliefs. For example, people are more likely to choose to engage in an activity to the extent that they see their involvement as leading to valued, positive outcomes (e.g., social and self-approval, tangible rewards, attractive work conditions, etc.)."[75]

For children of immigrants, the "consequences and outcomes" of pursuing an interest outside of medicine, law, or engineering are not immediately favorable. Their parents will almost instantly feel disappointed, or at the very least, concerned. For one who has learned to live for parental approval, leaving to pursue a side interest would be a near certain failure. Further, unlike medicine, law, and engineering where the path and results are fairly clear, the consequences of pursuing a novel interest might be much harder to predict.

Additionally, according the SCCT model, the interests that we develop are actually substantively connected to the manner and context in which we were raised:

"Over the course of childhood and adolescence, people are exposed, directly and vicariously, to a variety of occupationally relevant activities in school, at home, and in their communities. They are also deferentially reinforced for continuing their engagement, and for developing their skills, in different activity domains. The types and variety of activities to which children

75 "Social Cognitive Career Theory."

> and adolescents are exposed is partly a function of the context and culture in which they grow up. Depending on cultural norms, for example, girls are typically exposed to and reinforced for engaging in different types of activities than are boys."[76]

This phenomenon has definitely played out in my life; growing up, because of my culture, I believed that becoming a doctor, lawyer, or engineer was the *pinnacle* of success. Mentally, I couldn't conceive why that wouldn't be the case. For example, while I was in college, I knew that some people were gearing up for careers in consulting and banking. I would later find out that these fields are extremely lucrative and prestigious, but at the time, I felt since it wasn't medicine, law, or engineering, it probably wasn't worth exploring.

My mindset in college reminds me of a story that my dad frequently told us about an older woman from Nigeria. Her grandson had done well enough to purchase a used Bugatti Veyron, a sports car that retails for over two million dollars. But when the grandson showed the car to his grandmother, she was thoroughly unimpressed, asking, "What about a Mercedes or BMW?" To many immigrants, Mercedes and BMWs, like doctors, lawyers, and engineers, represent success. So, in the case of the grandmother, while the Bugatti may have had more value, it did not represent that value as well as a BMW would have.

---

76 Ibid.

Paramita Roy, a second-generation American working as a talent specialist and associate vice president for Bank Leumi, connects the lesson of this story to choosing a career path:

> "If you studied anthropology, and your mom is a big-time executive director at a bank, you're just going to know naturally from osmosis from your parents, that these jobs exist. But if your mom happens to work in a supermarket, and immigrated from a different country, she is not going to know these things, and neither will you."

However, all is not lost if you are no longer an adolescent and desire to change your path; the SCCT provides some support for the idea that our interests can develop later in life.

> "Interest development may be most fluid up until late adolescence, the point at which general interests (e.g., in art, science, social, or mechanical activities) tend to become fairly stable. At the same time, data on the stability of interests suggest that interest change does occur for some people during their post-adolescent years. SCCT posits that such changes, when they do occur, can be explained by changes in self-efficacy beliefs and/or outcome expectations—more precisely, by exposure to potent new learning experiences (e.g., parenting, technological advances, job training, or

restructuring) that enable people to alter their sense of self-efficacy and outcome expectations in new occupational and avocational directions."[77]

It's possible to develop and pursue new interests, whether in medicine, law, engineering, or elsewhere, and we will discuss how you can do so later in the book. But first, we let's learn from those who have come before us.

KEY TAKEAWAYS

- You may not be cognizant of your interests because your upbringing did not allow for exploration.
- The development of your interests is directly tied to that which your parents exposed you growing up.
- The extent to which you can envision a positive outcome for a particular path will determine your ability to pursue and succeed at a particular path.

77 "Social Cognitive Career Theory."

PART 2

POTENTIAL PATHS

In Part 2 we will cover five case studies of individuals who took different approaches to pursuing their dreams.

6

THE TALK

Temi Tuby-Lukan, a Columbia University chemical engineering graduate and current assistant procurement manager at Unilever provides us with an exemplary case study. Temi's story is a prime lesson in how to manage constant and seemingly unending criticism from your parents about the life you want to build.

"I'll never forget. I went home one weekend. . . I wish my sister had been home," Temi laughed and took a long pause. "And I told my parents, 'Sit down, let's chat.' After I told them they both were like, 'Are you okay? Was it something at work? Did something happen to you?'"

Without context, one could infer that Temi had told her parents one of the following things:

- She had lost custody of her children.
- She was in a car accident.
- She spent a night in jail.

But Temi has no children, didn't get into a car accident, and definitely didn't spend a night in jail. What Temi actually told her parents was that she wanted to take a gap year from working at Unilever to participate in AmeriCorps, a volunteer public service organization sponsored by the US government.

This moment is one that is familiar to most parents. Their child, brimming with curiosity and ambition, attempts to stretch their wings and explore their passions. They, as parents who are often conversely filled with skepticism and concern, are then forced to make a decision about how to respond to this attempt:

- Should I stop them because they don't know what they are getting into?
- Should I allow them so that they can be their own person?
- What if they get hurt?

All parents face these questions, but for many immigrant parents, there are often broader and more critical questions to answer:

- I'm in a new country and culture. How can I help my children navigate this unknown path if I'm still learning to navigate it myself?
- What if they fail and run out of money? I can't afford to support them.
- What will I tell my relatives and friends who believe I moved here so that my children could be successful?

These are challenging questions, often based in love, yet also in past experiences and fear.

After taking my leave of absence from law school, I moved to Seattle and began my first attempt at building a start-up company with a co-founder from Microsoft. Our business was called Mango, an on-demand therapy service (you can still see our website at joinmango.com). Although it was exhilarating to be chasing my dream, I wasn't making any money. I eventually decided to move home to save my remaining funds, and as you can imagine, tensions were high. My dad simply could not understand my time investment into something that didn't generate *any* money. Almost daily, he would tell me that when he arrived in the US, he had only a few hundred dollars to his name and no family to fall back on. He needed to figure out how to earn money by any means.

For immigrant parents, the desire to ensure the safety and success of their children is substantially higher than average. But regardless of their parents' fears, many children of immigrants do not share the same concerns. They spend their formative years in the United States, which exposes them to kids who are raised differently than they are. Plus, they do not experience the same hardships as their parents, creating a different level of concern around scarcity.

In Temi's case, while she was grateful for her role at Unilever, her operational position at the company was quite monotonous. As a chemical engineering major stretched to her intellectual limits on a daily basis, her experience is not surprising.

During her first year at Unilever, her regret of not studying abroad as an undergraduate began to stand out a bit more prominently. She had seen a number of her classmates travel to different countries, and so with each work email she sent, the urge to leave grew stronger and stronger.

> "After a point I was just like, 'Woah. . . am I just supposed to work for the rest of my life? I come in and do my tasks, I leave,'"
>
> TEMI REMARKED REGARDING HER EARLY EXPERIENCE AT UNILEVER.

I think many of us have had a job like this—a solid job with a solid paycheck, but a very not-solid sense of fulfillment or excitement. It leaves a lot of time to think about the "what ifs" and "maybe I coulds." So, naturally, Temi began to look for a way to alleviate her concerns.

"So the one thing that I landed on was that I just want to live somewhere else for a little bit without being tied down to that area. I want to do some service work; I want to do AmeriCorps."

In true engineer fashion, Temi did a lot of research on her available options prior to settling on AmeriCorps. She ran through theoretical scenarios of what the gap year would look like, addressing things such as how much money she would need and which locations would be feasible. Temi even went as far as designing and conducting prototype conversations with people who had done AmeriCorps in the past.

We'll discuss prototype conversations in much more detail in Part 3 of the book, but I'll quickly summarize it here. A prototype conversation is a tool created by Stanford professors Bill Burnett and Dave Evans as a way of getting a clearer idea of whether the job, hobby, or car you want is going to be a good fit for you without actually having to experience it yourself. Burnett explains the concept a bit more completely in this excerpt from his 2017 Ted Talk:

> "You know William Gibson, the famous science fiction writer, has a quote: 'The future is already here, it's just unevenly distributed.' That is, there is someone who is a bartender in Ibiza, and she has been doing it for years. I could go meet her and have a conversation. All these people are out there, they're living in my future. They're doing what I want to do, today. If I have a conversation with them and I just ask for their story—and everyone will tell you their story if you buy them a cup of coffee—and if I hear something in the story that rings in me. . . we have this thing called narrative resonance. When I hear a story that's kind of like my story, something happens. I can identify that as a potential way of moving forward."[78]

Temi had done this without even knowing about the concept of "prototype conversations." Her expensive Ivy League chemical engineering degree not only landed her at one of the most prominent companies in the world but also gave her

---

78 Bill Burnett, "Designing Your Life | Bill Burnett | TEDxStanford," TEDxTalks, May 19, 2017, YouTube video, 25:20.

the skills to attune, optimize, and manage the risks associated with the pursuit of her personal interests.

But despite all of Temi's research, she knew that telling her parents about this plan would not go well.

"I talked to my sister about it, and I was like, 'I am going to tell mommy and daddy that I want to do it.' My sister was like, 'You sure?'" Temi recounted. "Man, oh man. . ." she sighed.

This wasn't Temi's first time dealing with the scorn and disapproval of her parents; she has never been the type to say, "Oh because you said this, I am going to do this." Since childhood, she has always been analytical and intellectually independent.

"School was really, really easy for me. I always got good grades, no matter what. I could be sitting there being lazy, but my parents never yelled at me, never berated me because I always got As. Because what could they say, since I was already doing well?"

When she entered Columbia University to begin her chemical engineering degree, things changed. Although she's extremely glad she chose chemical engineering for the optionality it gave her, she acknowledges that it was extremely challenging, particularly because for the first time in her educational career, she had to learn how to study to get good grades.

Lena Nguyen, an admission's strategist at the University of Chicago's Laboratory Schools, explains the reason for the difficulties that Temi faced:

> "The major is an intersection between physics, chemistry, and math—three notoriously difficult subjects even on their own. Students have to master all three to gain a deep understanding of chemical engineering as a whole. The study of chemical engineering takes a lot of time, effort, and *conscious* attention. Because of its breadth, ChemE is perhaps the most time-intensive engineering major."[79]

However, Temi's parents were not aware of this unique difficulty associated with her degree program:

> "For the first two years or so of school, my Dad just kept berating me, acting like I wasn't taking school seriously. . . 'It's because you're not studying hard enough, you're not trying hard enough, and you're not paying attention.' But I was like, 'No, I just picked a hard major.' But he wouldn't believe it."

Once Temi's father heard from other parents and students who were familiar with the strenuous nature of the chemical engineering path, he began to believe that Temi was, in fact, working really hard.

But this was a warning for Temi; her independent thinking and processing would only be accepted as long as she produced results that were also acceptable. So, Temi knew from experience how the conversation would go when she told her parents about her AmeriCorps gap-year dream.

---

79 Lena Nguyen, "The Hardest Engineering Majors: A Detailed Guide for Overachievers," *College and Career (blog)*, Transizion, June 7, 2020.

In 2016, Temi found herself sitting in her parents' living room in a sleepy neighborhood of Malden, Massachusetts. With the sound of front porch chatter drifting through the windows, Temi dropped the news.

> "They just could not understand the idea. They were so shell-shocked. They both didn't talk to me for the rest of the day because they were just like, 'Why would you leave your job that's paying you money to do something for a year? What are people going to say afterward? They're going to see a year gap on your resume, for what? You want to do charity work. . . wait until you're thirty and then donate. What are you talking about?'"

Temi knew this moment would come, and she had prepared a reply:

"I was like, 'No, it's a really well-known program. I have enough money saved. . . I did my research, and I just feel like I'm still young—I'm twenty-three years old. It's going to be a blip. . . if there's a time for me to do something like this, it's now.'"

But her reply did little to assuage her parents' concerns.

"The next day my mom literally said that she went out to get food but she couldn't eat it because she couldn't understand what was wrong," Temi recalled.

Silence filled the Tuby-Lukan household through the evening and into the next day—a familiar sound for many children of immigrants who approach their parents about pursuing their own dreams as opposed to following their expected path. As we discussed in Part 1, immigrant parents often invest so much into preparing their child to succeed in America that "dream chasing" simply spells nothing more than disaster.

"The next day, after everyone slept it over, my dad came to me and said, 'You know, that really shocked us. I don't even know what to say. I don't understand why you would do it.' I tried to explain it to them, and we actually ended up having a conversation about stability."

Stability is often the elephant in the room when it comes discussing the pros and cons of pursuing one's dreams. As noted in NPR's podcast episode entitled "The Economics of Pursuing Your Dreams," stability, or perceived future stability, can be a huge determining factor in whether or not one successfully pursues their dreams.[80]

For Temi, stability—or a fear of lacking it—never was a concern:

"I always grew up with stability, so it's not something that I ever feared not having. 'I know I'll be okay,'" Temi explained to her dad, who noted her perspective but retorted with one of his own:

"Well, I don't have that mindset. I need to make sure that I'm always stable. I need to always have a job. I need to always

---

80 Adam Davidson and Alex Bloomberg, "The Tuesday Podcast: The Economics of Pursuing Your Dreams," December 14, 2010, in *Planet Money*, produced by Nick Fountain, Alexi Horowitz-Ghazi, Darian Woods and Alex Goldmark, podcast, MP3 audio, 22:09.

have a paycheck coming in, to make sure I can take care of everything."

Temi's dad's mindset is common among first-generation immigrants. For many, finding work is hard enough, so a source of income that won't dry up or disappear in a recession is arguably worth more than the money actually earned. Yet, Temi was not privy to the extent of the financial situation that her parents experienced in their youth.

"My sister and I had no clue that our parents were in so much debt." Temi would additionally learn that when her mother moved to America in the early '90s, things were so tight financially that early on all she could eat was sardines and bread.

With this context in mind, her parents' reactions begin to make more sense. If you've been harmed by something in the past like not having enough money, there's a good chance you'll urge your children with every bone in your body to avoid that situation as well. Temi echoed this understanding of her dad's reaction:

"Not that he regretted that we were always stable, but I think it made him fear that we were going to take risks because things had always been so stable."

But what were they so afraid of? What did they think would happen if she took a year off to do service work? Temi had an idea:

"They were also fearful that I would have a hard time coming back into the workforce. I wasn't worried about that because I

had Columbia University on my degree, and I had a job with a good company. I wasn't worried about that."

But her mother, an analyst at a large global bank, and her father, a director of finance at a nonprofit, certainly didn't share this sense of certainty.

"They're in much more old-school industries where you can't have a gap on your resume. That looks bad for you. And I was trying to explain to them that it's not like that anymore—that experience means a lot more—but it just really wasn't sticking with them."

So, Temi dropped the AmeriCorps plan. Her parents had won the battle, but for Temi, the war was far from over. Still feeling that itch to travel and after realizing how hard it would be to get a job in a different country without giving her parents a heart attack, Temi got a new job within Unilever based in Virginia. As someone from the northeast, Virginia was like a new country from a cultural perspective.

Temi's parents soon imposed their expectations for her career once again. This time, however, she would not be pressured. "When are you going to get your master's?" Temi's mother asked on one of her few visits back to Boston. Temi, remembering the last bout with her parents, paused and delivered a confident reply: "I'm good. I'll figure it out."

Temi explained to her mom that she wasn't opposed to going back to school, but unless they were going to foot the bill again, she wasn't going to make the expensive investment just for the sake of going back. "I have to know long term that I'm paying for something that is beneficial for me."

> "Because my sister got a Doctor of Pharmacy degree, my mom all of a sudden was like, 'What if you want to get a manager's role or something? They're going to look at you without a master's degree or an MBA and they'll see someone else who has one, and they're going to pick them. You're going to get picked over. Don't you want to become good? Don't you want to be a manager or something?' And I was just like, 'I never told you I wanted to be a CEO of anything. I never told you that I had all these high aspirations. *You're* putting that on *me*. *You're* projecting that on *me*. But I have never in my life stated that those are *my* desires. I'm thinking about what I like to do.'"

But Temi had another idea about why her mom pressured her: because her grandmother was pressuring her mom. Temi's grandmother is a former principal and teacher in Nigeria, and now owns a school in the city of Lagos. As a young woman, Temi's grandmother left her family to go to school because her father wouldn't allow it. As a result, she became a vocal advocate for education and always asked her granddaughter when she would go back to school to get her master's. Temi recalled, "I realized maybe that's why my mom was on my case. My grandmother was probably talking to my mom asking, 'Why hasn't she gone back yet? What's wrong with her?'"

So, perhaps this saga was the result of nothing more than a bad game of telephone. Nevertheless, Temi and her parents are now at a place where the game is coming to a close.

> "I think now [my parents] are starting to get it more because I keep climbing at work. I'll be transparent with you—I started in supply chain and I now work in procurement. I make close to six figures without a secondary degree. I keep getting promoted. I don't have a master's degree."

> "Even my sister says, 'I spent all these damn years in pharmacy school to barely make six figures. You didn't have to put in all those years and you're still making nearly six figures?' So, I think my parents have started to understand I'm making good money. I realized that money is their thing. Once they saw I could make good money, they knew I was on the right path."

Parents just want stability for their children. A six-figure salary says job stability, and at least seemingly, so does being a doctor, lawyer, or engineer. So, if you are going to take another path, particularly one that is not well-known to your parents, demonstrating that you can make a substantive income is one way to assuage their concerns.

I guess what they say is true: money talks.

With this conclusion, I asked Temi to share her advice for students and their parents who are in similar positions.

"I think you should consider that their desire for you is to be okay. I wouldn't say you should be like, 'Forget my parents, I'm going to do what I want to.' No, I wouldn't take it there," Temi advised with a lighthearted laugh. "But I think it's important

to appreciate and understand that they did a lot of work for you to have this opportunity."

She went on to explain, "With that, still pursue what you want. If it isn't a traditional path, just make sure you're going super hard so that you can become successful in it. I don't think that you have to follow their instructions or their desires, but be respectful of what they did and make sure you're putting in the work where you need to."

She continued, "Sometimes things don't go the way you planned. Once you're out in the real world, you realize there's only so much you can control. The least you can do is try to be in a place where you can financially take care of yourself. Sometimes that takes longer than you want, but you have to make sure you're constantly working toward a place where you're not financially dependent on your parents. They worked too hard to not see you bear the fruits of their labor. Sometimes your version of success is different from theirs, but as long as you're able to take care of yourself, you should pursue whatever you want."

Fair enough, Temi.

Fair enough.

KEY TAKEAWAYS

- Parents may have a difficult time understanding a plan that does not involve making money.

- If you're going on a non-traditional route, parents want to know that you are capable of making money and supporting yourself.
- Regardless of whether or not you are making money, do the work. Be respectful of the investment that your parents made in you.

7

FINISHING THE RACE.

Our next case study features Obinna Obineche, a Columbia University graduate who's currently enrolled in medical school. From the outside, Obinna has a similar story to mine: a successful Nigerian who's thriving, smiling, and making his parents proud, all at the same time. But there's more to this story.

Obinna, like me, is a public high school graduate. He worked hard in his classes, did what he was supposed to do, and aimed to get into the best schools he could. While the Ivy Leagues seemed a bit out of reach, he applied anyway, and they accepted his applications. Obinna's parents were ecstatic and prepared to pay for his undergraduate education at Columbia University. Several other schools gave him a full scholarship. Despite their lower-tier status, he was willing to attend one of these schools in order to spare his parents the $200,000 tuition bill. However, his parents "had the money" and were willing to invest in sending Obinna to the prestigious Ivy League university.

Obinna soon found out of course that this investment came with a term sheet. Obinna's parents wanted him to go into medicine and they were not shy about their demands. Admittedly, Obinna did find some appeal in pursuing the medical field, but unlike his parents, he wasn't 100 percent sold. With his competency in math and science, he thought about biomedical engineering, computer science, or economics as alternatives to the traditional pre-med track. Nevertheless, when Obinna approached his parents about these other potential majors, they met him with a high level of resistance. This was a battle that wouldn't finish easily.

> "My parents definitely had a stern talking with me," Obinna remembered with a laugh. His parents said, "If you're even considering medicine, you should try it out, start with that, and see if that can work for you because we feel that it's a good life, it's good work, and it's going to give you job safety—you'll never be out of a job."

Although neither of Obinna's parents have worked in the medical field, what they said has some truth to it; doctors frequently rank highly on lists for job security.[81] Additionally, if you find a specialty that you like, it can truly be rewarding, fulfilling, and high-paying work.[82]

---

81 "10 Professions with the Best Job Security," MarketWatch, January 29, 2016.

82 Kevin Jubbal M.D., "5 Happiest Types of Doctors," Med School Insiders, November 10, 2019.

Obinna didn't put up much of a fight after that conversation and began the pre-med track. Let's not forget—despite his hard work in high school, Obinna was willing to choose a significantly lower-ranked college to spare his parents an expensive tuition bill. He, like many first-generation children, is accustomed to putting the interests of his parents before his own. This is not surprising. What *is* surprising is what happened to Obinna once he arrived at Columbia and began his journey to become a doctor.

> "You get there, and you realize, 'Wow, yes I'm intelligent and my test scores and grades tell me that I belong here, but there's definitely a difference.' Especially in that pre-med environment where it's like, 'Wow, I am not quite as prepared as some of my peers and I'm finding myself feeling like I have to work a lot harder to get certain things."

Richard J. Light, a Harvard professor and higher education policy expert, alongside his colleagues at Georgetown, Duke, and Brown are working to find out how first-generation students fare compared with others.

While their research is not yet complete, some evidence shows that "many first-generation freshmen hadn't anticipated feeling less prepared than classmates," which has mental and social consequences. There are also tangible outcomes in the form of grades: "Typically, first-generation freshman GPAs lag behind their peers' by 0.3 points."[83]

---

83 Laura Pappano, "First-Generation Students Unite," *New York Times*, April 8, 2015.

These realities hit Obinna particularly hard, leaving him with less than stellar grades and a lot of concerns about whether or not he should continue along the pre-med track. "A lot of people who came in pre-med pivoted out and are working in finance or working in consulting," he remarked.

But when Obinna approached his parents again about his grade situation and desire to take another path, they were less than happy.

> "At least for my parents, there's an idea that specifically in healthcare there's a greater level of job security in that space. For them that's the key thing. They see people who work in other sectors, and they are like, 'Oh, you could lose your job and what happens?'"

Obinna let out a short sigh and continued:

> "But if you're working at a large consulting firm or a big bank, you most likely are making really good money and have a lot of marketable skills. If you do happen to lose your job, you can get back on your feet relatively quickly, especially if you have the pedigree of Columbia behind you. But I think that gets lost."

The data seems to support Obinna's claim; Michael Gibson, the VP of Grants for the Thiel Foundation, points out that "in 2010 close to 36 percent of Princeton graduates with full-time jobs went into finance, down from a pre-financial crisis high of 46 percent in 2006, but still more than one-third of an entire class. If you add management consulting to the count, it's more than 60 percent. Likewise, graduates from

Harvard are more likely to enter finance and consulting than all other career paths."[84]

These statistics aren't shocking considering how much the schools emphasize these career paths. For example, our alma mater Columbia literally has a Goldman Sachs-sponsored room in the career services office.

Gibson continues: "For any given Ivy grad, getting a job in professional services makes good practical sense. The money is good, the action exciting, the high-status intoxicating. It's a career with optionality."[85]

Obinna is touching on something that many first-generation kids understand: their parents have a limited view of what success and stability in America can look like. In Obinna's case, his parents' limited view produced a lot of external pressure that made him continue along the pre-med path despite knowing that it probably wasn't the right fit. And according to Obinna, this pressure may have done him more harm than good.

> "If I didn't have the familial push or pressure to go into medicine, I probably would've pivoted into something else, and I think I would have been in a more comfortable position at this stage in my life. Because now, I'm in my second year of medical school, pushing along, and going to have a lot of debt."

---

84 Michael Gibson, "The Ivy League Has Perfected the Investment Banker and Management Consultant Replicator," *Forbes*, February 7, 2014.

85 Ibid.

Obinna and I shared a nervous, yet understanding chuckle as he continued, "It's going to be a while before I'm making the physician's salary that my skills and knowledge would merit."

> "But looking back, if I wanted to just work and build up that way and move from company to company, I would be very comfortable financially. My parents paid for undergrad so I wouldn't have any debt and would be on a fast track to doing something else—maybe working for a while, saving up some funds, and possibly going to business school or something instead."

It seemed like Obinna had a pretty clear idea that there were potentially more profitable avenues for success, so an obvious question remained:

Why was he still doing it?

Was it simply the familial pressure that caused him to not only study medicine for four years at Columbia, but also take out substantial student loans to pursue a medical degree?

"For me it's really just the overall cost—the amounts of time and effort I've put in. The literal cost in the sense of loans taken out, and if I pivot, I'm still going have that sitting on me. And then after years of being on this path there's just a desire in some ways to see it through."

Regardless of what pushed him to stay the course in medicine, he's done a lot of labor and spent a lot of money. I can relate to this; when I was considering taking a leave of absence from school, I looked back at all the years I spent studying and preparing applications and felt like it would be a huge waste if I just walked away. Ultimately, it's hard to make an about-face and acknowledge that all of your previous work may have been for nothing. This situation is popularly known as the sunk-cost fallacy and, despite its name, the research shows that it may be a useful strategy.[86]

But as I pressed Obinna further, I realized that something else was driving his decision to continue:

"The other thing is that I've been on such a specific, unilateral path that even if I wanted to just jump ship and do something else, I'd need to put in a ton of time and energy into reconstructing things."

So, beyond the fear of facing a sunk cost, he was also concerned about the time and effort he'd have to expend to study and prepare for another field.

I asked Obinna how all of this made him feel. He replied,

> "I personally hate school. I don't love school at all. But there's a sizable kernel of interest in the work itself that I would actually be able to do once I finish. It's just that it's such a long road that it does get frustrating at times. But I just try and stay patient and keep plugging along, because if I become a doctor then I'll be able to do something I feel still has substance and

86 Ryan Doody, "The Sunk Cost 'Fallacy' Is Not A Fallacy," *Ergo: An Open Access Journal of Philosophy* 6 (2020): 1153-1190.

> merit—I'll be doing good work, impacting people, and using these skills I put a lot of time into."

Although his parents may have won this battle, there's some hope that Obinna will eventually find joy in his career.

I asked him what his advice would be to other students who are considering the medical field:

> "So, along the path of trying to pursue medicine, you run into all of these mentor types. There are the older doctors, and every once in a blue moon I'd meet a black male that happened to be in medicine. I actually have a mentor now who I still turn to and is one of the few black doctors I have on speed dial. He was always tough on me, questioning, 'Are you sure you want to do this?'"

Obinna pointed out that this kind of questioning about entering medical school was the norm for older doctors. At the time, he thought it was people questioning his capability to secure the degree; in retrospect, he realized that they simply were trying to make sure that he fully understood what he was getting into.

> "Your life as you know it is never going to be the same once you enter medical school," Obinna continued. "You're going have a lot of debt and your earning potential is going to essentially be capped, whereas if you go into fields like business, finance, or tech, there's a lot of different avenues to be successful."

"Knowing all of that, I wouldn't necessarily tell a kid, 'No, don't do medicine.' I don't know him. I don't know what drives him—maybe it's his parents, maybe it's him, and maybe it's a combination of both. I would just say to take the time to get a very good sense of exactly what you're getting into. Try to shadow a lot of different specialties, and maybe scribe. You need to do work in the field as much as possible. And you'll hear other people give this advice too, and it may seem like they just want you to have experience for your resume. But you really need to see what that work looks like."

KEY TAKEAWAYS

- Parents may lack awareness about other career paths that are more profitable, less demanding, and virtually as stable as medicine, law, and engineering.
- When people push back against you pursuing medicine, it's likely not because they don't think you're capable—it's because they want you to know exactly how challenging the work is.
- Do everything you can to learn what it's actually like to be a doctor. It's not about your resume. It's about getting a deep understanding.

8

ACTING DIFFERENT

"I ask myself everyday: Am I doing the right thing? Am I? Because more than anything. . . more than anything in the world, I want to be good."

These are the words of the subject of our next case study: first-generation Indian American Neha Sobti. Against the wishes of her parents, Neha decided not to enroll in law school. Her story points out some of the ways that pursuing your dream can have social implications for your parents.

After interning for a few law firms and realizing law wasn't for her, Neha instead decided to move across the country to become an actress in Los Angeles; the above quote is actually a line from a role for which she's auditioning.

For many first-generation children like Neha, the idea of eschewing a stable and prestigious career such as law for a highly improbable one like acting is extremely painful and isolating.

In Neha's case, forgoing law school to become an actress brought up one main issue: reputation. But it was not her reputation that was the problem—it was that of her parents. Prior to moving to LA, Neha had graduated from the prestigious Georgetown University with a degree in sociology. Her parents had much to brag about when it came to Neha's achievements, especially because of her plan to attend law school.

But when Neha changed course, so did her parents' tone:

> "In Indian culture, they really care about what other people think, and so the first thing my mom said was, 'What am I going to tell other people? What about our reputation?'"[87]

This reaction wasn't exactly a ringing endorsement. The decision to reveal a personal dream is, at a minimum, a vulnerable and unnerving experience. In an ideal world, you'd reveal your dream to someone who's caring, encouraging, and able to help you find a way to pursue that dream. Unfortunately, that's not the easiest role for most parents to play, much less an immigrant parent who's still trying to navigate a new society.

---

87 "I Quit Law School to Become an Actress | L.A. Land | Refinery29," April 14, 2018, YouTube video, 7:41.

While it's reasonable to expect that the average parent would first be concerned with their child and their change of heart, for Neha and for many other first-generation kids, this isn't a reasonable expectation.

First-generation children are often raised with the understanding that their lives are not necessarily *theirs* and that they have certain career and personal expectations to fulfill in order receive support from their families. A lot of these expectations stem from the fact that many immigrant cultures operate from a collectivist lens as opposed to the more individualist lens that dominates the west.

> "Collectivist cultures emphasize the needs and goals of the group as a whole over the needs and desires of each individual. In such cultures, relationships with other members of the group and the interconnectedness between people play a central role in each person's identity," writes Kendra Cherry, author of *The Everything Psychology Book*.[88]

Cultures in Asia, Central America, South America, and Africa tend to be more collectivistic, resulting in a different set of behaviors and concerns at an individual level.[89]

Some of the common traits of collectivist cultures include:

- Primary focus on selflessness and putting community needs ahead of individual needs.

---

88 Kendra Cherry, "Understanding Collectivist Cultures," VeryWellMind, accessed March 24, 2020.

89 Ibid.

- Group work over individual work.
- Family and community playing a central role in decision making.
- Common goals being given greater emphasis than individual pursuits.[90]

As a result, members of these cultures frequently look down upon behaviors that are self-serving and don't benefit the larger familial structure. This mindset is also shown in the way that those from collectivist cultures describe themselves; research suggests that while those raised in individualistic cultures frequently refer to themselves in terms of personality traits and characteristics (e.g., I'm smart, honest, and funny), those raised in more collectivistic cultures refer to themselves in terms of their relationships (e.g., I'm a good brother, son, and friend).[91]

As such, Neha's decision to pursue her dream at the expense of her parents' concerns looks different depending on the perspective from which it's viewed. If viewed through an individualistic lens, Neha is exercising her individuality by admirably building a life reflective of her interests, not those of her parents. If viewed through a collectivist lens, however, Neha's behavior could be considered selfish and disrespectful of the central role that family plays in one's life.

The implications of this difference for children of immigrants cannot be understated. Unlike our parents, we've grown up having to balance the expectations of two different worlds. On the one hand, the elite institutions that we're encouraged

---

90 Ibid.

91 Ibid.

to enter have an unambiguous preference for independent thought and following your own interests. In fact, I recall one piece of advice I received while trying to decide whether or not I should go to law school: "Grow a pair, stop listening to your parents, and do what you want with your life."

On the other hand, we have a cultural understanding that being a good person and prioritizing the interests of the family go hand in hand; growing up, every time my siblings and I received a paycheck, we had to give each member of the family a cut of our earnings. The idea was that the things you earn on your own will always be for your family, too.

Because of this difference, for children of immigrants, the decision to pursue a dream in some ways forces your family to come along on your journey to your dream as well. In fact, in Neha's case, her parents felt such shame that they didn't tell anyone about her decision to become an actress until two years after she moved to Los Angeles. After they told the rest of the family, things got worse.[92]

> "I have kind of become the black sheep of the family. I don't even talk to my one grandfather who was like, 'Oh, that's not a profession. How can you give up your college education for this?' He was just going off."[93]

92 "I Quit Law School to Become an Actress."

93 Ibid.

Neha points out that she's learned how to tune him out, but her grandfather still tells her mom, "This is your fault. You raised her like this."[94]

With tears in her eyes, Neha acknowledges that watching her parents get the brunt of the blame for her decisions is hard to handle. While Neha's social circle—likely composed of those who were reared in an individualistic culture—may be cheering her on, the same cannot be said for that of her parents; their social circle feels that Neha's parents have failed her and that she's brough shame to the family. Again, from a collectivist lens, Neha's actions can be considered egregious offenses.

The question still remains: what's so bad about what Neha is doing? How can a twenty-two-year-old who's pursuing her dreams be considered reputation-damaging? Why does Neha's grandfather believe that she was raised improperly simply because she wants to become an actress? The answers are complex, but according to Neha, the reason why there's such an issue again boils down to just one word: stability.

"I know that the best way to prove them [wrong] is to just earn a stable paycheck and show my dad that I can make a career of this."[95]

As we have discussed, for many immigrant parents, careers such as law, medicine, and engineering provide a clear path to financial stability while also furnishing them with a

---

94 Ibid.

95 Ibid.

commensurate level of pride from the moment their child begins preparing applications.

Acting, however, doesn't often meet any of these criteria. According to the Bureau of Labor Statistics, the median pay for an actor is $20.43 per hour, and "most actors have long periods of unemployment between roles."[96] While there's a possibility of Neha becoming famous and arguably bringing pride and a positive reputation to her parents, the odds of her becoming even a C-list celebrity are slim.[97]

Yvonne Orji, the child of two Nigerian immigrants, is a famous comedian and actress on the HBO series *Insecure*. She's pointed out why her mom had such an issue when she decided to give up on medical school to pursue her career in comedy.

> "My mom definitely cried. My mom just immediately cried. Tears were shed. I'm also the youngest of four, so I was like the last black hope in terms of her getting a doctor. So, it was just like, 'Wait a minute, I don't have any other kids left.' .... She saw herself getting on a plane in 1988 to come to America and wishing she never got on that plane. It was like, 'How do I reset the clock so that this chick cannot disappoint me?'"[98]

---

96 *Occupational Outlook Handbook*, s.v. "Actor," accessed September 25, 2020.

97 Jim Hanas, "You Are Not Going to Be Famous," *New York Post*, July 25, 2009.

98 "Yvonne Orji of 'Insecure' on Becoming a Comedian: 'My Mom Definitely Cried'," Associated Press, June 10, 2020, YouTube video, 2:54.

But as Yvonne said in her recent HBO stand-up special, now that she has a thriving career, her mother is more than happy to tout Yvonne's successes. "These days, if you catch my mom today it's a different story: 'Do you have HBO? Home. Box. Office. Yes, that is where my daughter is.'"[99]

Taking Yvonne's story into account, it seems understandable that Neha's decision to pursue her acting dream met so much resistance. It's not necessarily that she's pursuing her dream that's the problem; had Neha told her parents that she had an epiphany that she'd be happier as a doctor and that she was going to take a few years to study for the MCAT, Neha would've likely been met with cheers and praise.

Perhaps, the issue is really that Neha's dream is unlikely to come true. Doctors, lawyers, and engineers do not face the same statistical odds. They have a set path. If they work hard, pass the courses, and take on a lot of debt, they'll become a doctor, lawyer, or an engineer. In fact, when studying for the LSAT, the MCAT, or engineering exams, your parents can begin bragging in advance that you're going to become a doctor, lawyer, or engineer. So much certainty exists in the paths to these careers that if you tell someone what you're going to be, they have no real reason to doubt you.

Outcome: certain.

There's no set path to becoming a famous actress, however. It's basically a crap shoot that requires a combination of luck, bullheaded determination, and years and years of rejection.

99 Ibid.

As actor Soren Bowie points out:

> "Any struggling actors who have never had a significant role before are not members of the Screen Actors Guild. SAG was designed as a union to ensure that actors were paid fair wages for their work. Nearly every movie and television show has to operate within the guidelines of SAG, which means that they can only hire SAG actors or else they have to pay a hefty fine to cast someone outside the union. Naturally, studios will cast SAG members over nonmembers every time. So how do you become a member? Well, that's where things get completely absurd.
>
> The rules of SAG state, 'Performers are eligible to join Screen Actors Guild after working on a SAG film in a principal role.' So, just to clarify, no one will cast you unless you are already in the union, and you can't get into the union until you are cast. A director has to like you so much that he or she is willing to trust you with a primary role despite the fact that you have no previous experience in film *and* be willing to pay a fine just to have you in that role."[100]

Outcome: uncertain.

Now it's a bit easier to understand the response from Neha's family. From the collectivist lens, choosing to pursue her dream as an actress—which is highly unlikely to pan out—is a selfish move that harms the family's reputation.

---

100 Hanas, "You Are Not Going to Be Famous."

It was no surprise that when I asked Neha for her advice to students in her position, she said, "If you can see yourself potentially being happy as a doctor, lawyer, or engineer, you should do that. But if you feel you cannot be happy without pursuing your dream, then you have to go for it."

KEY TAKEAWAYS

- The differences between collectivistic thinking and individualistic thinking can serve as a source of conflict between what you want and what your parents want.
- The reason why parents often push a career in medicine, law, or engineering is because there's a clear path to entering the field, unlike in professions such as acting.
- If you believe you can carve out a happy life in the career your parents want for you, it may be a good idea to follow that path. However, if you believe your happiness can only come from following your personal dream, you should pursue it.

9

DIFFERENT PERSPECTIVES

Most kids have dreams:

Astronaut.
Princess.
Rapper.
Rockstar.
Athlete.

The subject of our next case study, Paramita Roy, also had a dream as a kid:

Having her own room.

Paramita, a graduate of Barnard College, explained further:

"I grew up not having as much money as I wanted as a kid. I always had this dream of having my own room and owning a home, so financial stability has always been important to

me. So, I never really dreamed of going into a profession that wasn't lucrative or wouldn't pay bills."

Paramita is now a talent acquisition specialist and associate vice president at Bank Leumi USA and makes an extremely comfortable salary. She made her dream come true.

However, as the daughter of two immigrant parents from Bangladesh, her path to this lucrative role didn't come without a fight. To make ends meet, her mother worked as a cashier at a supermarket and her father worked as a concierge. Her parents immigrated with clear intentions for their children to achieve success and become either a doctor, a lawyer, or an engineer.

"At the beginning, it was definitely 'Be a lawyer, be a doctor, be an engineer,' but as time went on. . . as I was trying to figure out what I wanted to do, I realized pretty quickly that I wanted to pivot and do something else," said Paramita.

PARAMITA, TALENT ACQUISITION SPECIALIST AND AVP

In addition to being excited about having her own room, Paramita was enthusiastic about math and science as a kid. As a result, she thought that she would follow a path to engineering.

"My parents were really excited about that, but then I took Calc 4 at Columbia and I was like, 'Oh my god I am going to die. A 2.5 GPA? I'm not going to make it out alive.'"

So, Paramita decided to switch from her highly rigorous math major to psychology, something a bit easier and more aligned with what she'd later find out is her natural skill set: connecting with people and helping others.

The switch, at least initially, had less to do with her interest in the mind and had a lot more to do with realizing her dream. She concluded that if she was going to accomplish her dream of having a lucrative job, then she would need to be employable. A 2.5 GPA simply wasn't going to cut it.

But for Paramita's parents, the switch signaled nothing short of disaster.

> "I tell my mom that I'm going to study psychology so I can have a great GPA and get a job when I graduate. And my mom—you should have seen her face—she literally turned blue. Whenever I would come home during weekends or breaks, my mom would wake me up in the middle of the night and be like, 'Paramita, you were a math major. You should go back to that. Are you sure you're going to have a job?'"

Paramita could clearly see that there was another path to financial security and that persevering through the math major would likely lead to her struggling for even a decently paying job after graduation.

Her parents, however, couldn't see things from Paramita's perspective.

> "I think it's this fear of not having job security. Because you know, for my parents, if you aren't studying science, there are no jobs. It was very black and white. But they don't know," Paramita remarked lovingly, as if talking about her children. "They don't know what's out there. They just want some sort of stability."

As we have seen, stability is a common theme.

Parents want financial security and stability for their kids but have a limited view of the ways of procuring them. For example, in my senior year of college, I told my dad that I was going to take some time off before law school to work. Like any good student, I had read all the blogs and talked to all the advisors, and everyone seemed to agree that getting some work experience under my belt would be helpful. I'd have more time to improve my application and a chance to see what life in a big law firm was like.[101] When I told him this, he had a lot of resistance and urged me to just apply and go straight after college. He thought that the faster I got through school, the better off I'd be.

Paramita argues that the reason why this happens is because our parents, having immigrated from a different country, have a limited view of what paths to success are available.

---

101 Gabriel Kuris, "How to Choose Between Applying to Law School, Taking a Gap Year," *U.S. News & World Report*, accessed October 1, 2020.

Research supports this idea. According to a study led by researchers at the University of Nebraska:

> "Many recent immigrants and refugees will be unaware of career options available to them... Similar to how the children and adolescents who are born in the United States face barriers in their career development from lack of adequate information, so too do recent immigrant and refugee adults. Lack of knowledge may result in low self-efficacy and low-outcome expectation. It may indeed be one of the biggest barriers to career development of individuals within this group."[102]

Fortunately for Paramita, the career department at Barnard helped open her eyes to these alternative opportunities. "I remember going to Barnard's career development, and they were like, 'You should try H...R.' And I was like, 'What's H...R.?' I had no idea," Paramita remarked, chuckling softly. "And they said, 'Oh, it's human resources. You hire people, you fire people, and you help them grow within corporations.' Then, a lightbulb went off in my head."

While many people primarily think of human resources as the place you go when starting and leaving a job, or when you need to file a work complaint there's much more to it. Harvard Business School graduates Matthew D. Breitfelder and Daisy Wademan Dowling explain:

---

102 Oskana Yakushko et al., "Career Development Concerns of Recent Immigrants and Refugees," *Journal of Career Development* 24, no. 4 (Summer 2008): 362–396. Accessed October 9, 2020.

> "A career in human resources isn't the typical destination of a Harvard MBA. We're supposed to be employed as strategy consultants or investment bankers or, in the true spirit of the degree, general managers. We once had jobs like those, but we don't now, and we know what our classmates are thinking: 'It's a work-life balance thing.' 'They don't have the stomach for *real* business.' 'If you can't do, teach.' And, of course, our favorite: 'If they're so interested in helping people, why don't they just go into social work?' Well, the answer is simple—and we relish providing it. HR today sits smack-dab in the middle of the most compelling, competitive battleground in business, where companies deploy and fight over that most valuable of resources—workforce talent."[103]

After visiting career services, Paramita discovered a path not only to financial stability but also to a job she enjoyed, all without laboring through her math major and becoming an engineer. She completed her degree at Barnard and, after interviewing on campus for a few different HR positions, landed a job at the headquarters for the popular retail chain Macy's.

As Paramita would find out, however, there was a force at work other than the importance of stability: the importance of reputation. "So, it's interesting. . . because I had accepted a job at the headquarters of Macy's, there was this stigma among my South Asian community that I was working at the *store*." According to Paramita, they made this assumption because

103 Matthew D. Breitfelder and Daisy Wademan Dowling, "Why Did We Ever Go Into HR?," *Harvard Business Review*, published July 1, 2008.

Macy's hires so many South Asian people as sales associates. "They couldn't understand that there was this other thing."

Paramita's parents would try to defend her in public by clarifying that she was working at the head office. Despite their explanations, the disconnect was so large that others from Paramita's temple in New York simply couldn't understand the significance of her role. As a result, Paramita's parents received many disrespectful remarks such as, "She went to Barnard, and *that's* what she amounted to?"

Reputational importance is a common theme amongst first-generation immigrants. If stability is most important, then reputation follows closely behind.

As Tam Nguyen, a medical school graduate turned nail salon owner, remarked, his mother's dreams went beyond economic self-sufficiency. "Their American dream was for their son to be a physician and to bring honor, prestige, and a great living," Tam says. Tam's mother pointed out, wincing as she recalled the moment, "Well, yeah, of course most Vietnamese families want their kid to be a doctor or a lawyer, you know? We are the same. We have only one son."[104]

Paramita couldn't agree more, pointing out that despite objectively excelling in her career and making a comfortable salary greater than her parents' combined income, she still receives indicators that there's something wrong with her profession of choice.

---

104 Tam Ngyuen, "Nailing the American Dream, With Polish," interview by Karen Grigsby Bates, *All Things Considered*, NPR, June 14, 2012, audio, 7:00.

"Even still to this day there are people at the temple who I bump into who will be like, 'Oh Barnard, oh Columbia, what do you do?' And I'll be like, 'I work in HR. I hire people.' And they will just respond, 'That's disappointing.'"

Fortunately for Paramita, it seems as though her parents may have started to come around:

"But my parents will remind me, 'Those people don't actually know what you do. You actually make money, so just forget them. They're not going to pay the bills, so forget them.'"

That said, Paramita's parents haven't completely shaken their desire for prestige. "My parents still think I have to go and get a master's degree. They hound me about this master's degree because they think it's a higher indicator of success, and I am just like, 'In *what*? What do you want me to get a master's degree in?" she remarked with a lighthearted laugh.

I asked Paramita what could be driving such behavior at this point. She explains,

"This is a result of parents wanting to be able to say, 'Oh look, my kid. She has a master's degree while your kid has no master's degree.' And I'm looking at my parents like, this master's degree you're thinking of is going to cost me at least a hundred thousand dollars." That's an expensive amount for the sake of bragging rights.

"But then my parents will get excited and they'll go, 'Well, you can work and get the master's degree.' And I just look at them like, 'What am I going to get a master's degree in?' I think

they've dropped it, but it comes up sometimes. I think my parents think they're going to kill two birds with one stone."

Specifically, Paramita's parents think they'll not only get some personal prestige from the degree but will also help their daughter further advance in her career.

According to Paramita, she's thought about the prospect of it, but is certainly in no rush.

Paramita has found a way to both earn an impressive salary and be fulfilled without laboring through a math degree that she didn't like. The stability of her profession is also apparent; due to the Coronavirus, Paramita's former company, Even Financial, laid her off, but she had another high paying job at Bank Leumi within six weeks.

I asked her to share her advice for other parents and kids who are in a similar situation to hers. She said,

> "A lot of parents worry about their kids' future. They worry about their kids failing in life, just not doing well, or not being a doctor, lawyer, or engineer. I've heard so many parents say, 'Oh my gosh they're going to a liberal arts school. How are they going to become an engineer?'"

> "My advice to them would be, look, I'm a recruiter, and I have been doing this for five years. I don't just hire doctors, lawyers, and engineers. There are a lot of jobs out there. Take it from me—I hire people for a living. If your kid is very inspirational and likes to write, they

can be an account manager or account executive. They can sell software, and it's not like selling things at a supermarket. It's a very difficult job. You can be a data analyst and pull reports. You can work in HR. If you'd like you can literally email me at paramita314@gmail.com and I'll send you a list, and I can actually send you the job prospects too, just to calm your nerves."

KEY TAKEAWAYS

- Research shows that immigrant parents tend to have a more limited view of what career paths their children can choose in which to succeed.
- If you believe you can have more success by changing professions, your parents may not understand or support you, but that does not mean it is the wrong move.
- Many of immigrant parents' concerns have to do with reputation. You can assuage some of these concerns by demonstrating your ability to generate income.

3

WALKING THE WALK

In Part 3, we'll talk through how to take the next steps in your journey.

10

UNLAWFULLY WEDDED

Before we get into the practical advice, I must make an important clarification; In reality, the hierarchy of "doctor, lawyer, or engineer" in most immigrant families is actually "doctor, engineer, or lawyer." While law is undoubtedly a complex and difficult field and certain specializations like intellectual property can get highly technical, it's the one career that does not have any real pre-requisites—you simply need to be smart and hard-working. As such, when kids are unsure of what they want to do but are smart and driven, law school is often an appealing option.

While a job in the legal field seems stable and promising in theory, that's not always true in practice according to Aubrey Jones, a senior executive search consultant for Lucas Group, a high-end legal talent agency. Aubrey uses her deep expertise and knowledge of the legal market to match talented lawyers with law firms and corporate legal departments.

As someone who examines legal talent for a living, Aubrey is certainly qualified to give an opinion on the value of a legal degree in the modern era. But there's another reason why

Aubrey is so certain in her opinion that law is not the panacea of stability and economic enrichment that many believe it to be: Aubrey was a corporate lawyer in the midst of the 2008 financial crisis. When the crisis hit, the already racially and gender-insensitive firm environment she had endured worsened, and to protect her sanity, she left.

"There are a lot of stereotypes that go along with large law firm practice, for a very good reason," remarked Aubrey.

Large law firm practice, popularly known as "big law," is the dream for most students who seek a six-figure payday upon graduation.[105] But as Aubrey experienced, minority lawyers in these environments can face some difficult discrimination.

> "One of the comments that a partner gave me while I was a practicing attorney was that I would be great for a job like a Starbucks manager because I'm so good with people. There was also the issue of being an African American female. People would often assume that I was a paralegal, or even a secretary, even though my office had my name on it."

Aubrey found that even within her own practice group they struggled to see her as even a basic member of the team.

> "The head of my practice group came up to me at an event for the summer associates. I was very involved with the summer program—I participated and

105 "What is BigLaw, and why is it in danger?" Howstuffworks, accessed September 6, 2020.

answered the associates' questions when they needed help—and the head of the litigation group came up to me and introduced herself to me, even though I was currently working for her. She said the reason why she didn't recognize me was because my hair was in a ponytail. There was a lot of that."

Aubrey experienced these kinds of social slights as well as discriminatory behaviors routinely.

"If I made a mistake, I was written up and would never work for that partner again. Other people in my class—mostly white men—if they made a mistake, the partner fixed it and they would be like, 'This is just what happens.' I didn't have that thing where someone saw me as their daughter, or their niece, or someone they cared for, so I wasn't afforded those same privileges."

Aubrey isn't imagining these things.

According to a study by Nextions, "Supervising lawyers are more likely than not to perceive African American lawyers as having subpar writing skills in comparison to their Caucasian counterparts," a perception often due to confirmation bias.[106]

Confirmation bias is "the tendency to search for, interpret, favor, and recall information in a way that confirms or strengthens one's prior personal beliefs or hypotheses."[107]

---

106 Arin Reeves, "Written in Black & White - Exploring Confirmation Bias in Racialized Perceptions of Writing Skills" *Nextions, (2014).*

107 *Encyclopaedia Britannica Online*, Academic ed., s.v. "Confirmation Bias," accessed September 5, 2020.

Nextions' study found that "when expecting to find fewer errors, we find fewer errors. When expecting to find more errors, we find more errors."[108]

Although Aubrey was able to successfully land on her feet as an executive search consultant, because of these experiences, her advice for prospective law students is resolute and clear:

> "Anyone who is going to law school should go there because they know they want to practice. It's not the type of education that you go into because you're not sure what you want to do but you want to have a graduate degree."

Why? Well, for one, law school is expensive. Really expensive. The average student will graduate with at least $115,000 in debt.[109]

The average student also will graduate with a job that pays substantially less than $115,000.

"Due to a number of factors, and the way that the practice of law has changed overtime, the distance between what an average lawyer makes, and a big firm lawyer makes is

---

108 Reeves, "Written in Black & White."

109 "Is Law School Worth It Anymore?" Investopedia, accessed September 6, 2020.

large—extremely large," said Aubrey. "Most lawyers aren't making what people imagine—or what TV lawyers make."

Many of us have watched the popular television show *Suits*. If you haven't, here is the basic gist: gleaming marble offices with floor to ceiling windows overlooking New York City, fiery debates about court cases, black Mercedes with personal drivers, and casual outings to the opera.

While there are certainly some lawyers who live this life, it is, for the most part, an elusive fantasy.

> "Public defenders make between $50,000 and $60,000. Same thing with insurance lawyers. The number of people making those $190,000+ salaries coming out of school is extremely small, in the grand scheme of things. Additionally, the cost of education has gone up exponentially. So, it's just a really expensive bet to take if you're not sure that you want to practice."

Not only is it an expensive bet, but it's also likely to be a losing one if you're not sure about law school.

First, your grades stay with you for the rest of your career. According to Aubrey, your grades will not only determine employability at any point during your legal career, but they will also determine whether or not you'll have any stability or longevity in the profession.

Even for attorneys who graduated from law school five to eight years ago, law firms still pay a significant amount of attention to their law school grades when making hiring decisions.

> "I know someone who went to Georgetown. He graduated around the time of the recession or mid-recession. He graduated with a 2.8 GPA and couldn't get a job. He never ended up practicing because when things are lush and money is growing on trees, its fine. But when money is tight, they get really picky. That's when the nastiness comes out in people. So, they're going to be happy that you graduated from that top-tier school, but you're also going to need to prove yourself by having the good grades. I mean, my friend who graduated with a 2.9 isn't stupid; he got into Georgetown. But he never ended up practicing, and now he works for an alcohol company," Aubrey remarked.

You might be thinking, "I did well in high school and college. I'll be fine."

In law school, however, there's something infamously known as "the curve." The curve is the permitted range of each letter grade that can be awarded. It's "the main source of this competition" in law schools and "affects the class rank, affects the chances of making law review, affects the chances of scoring that big job/externship."[110]

The curve generally prevents students from excelling in law school on innate intelligence alone; in order to perform well, one must learn an entirely new method of writing and analysis and use their complete mental focus to make it to the top of the class.

---

110 Glesner Fines "Competition and the Curve," UKMC, accessed September 6, 2020.

Second, even if you have perfect grades, legal practice is nothing like what you see on television.

"When working at a law firm, the things that you learn in law school have very little to do with practicing. Law school teaches you how to think, but it doesn't teach you how to practice," said Aubrey.

Additionally, there's also the risk—particularly as a minority—that you'll face an environment similar to what Aubrey confronted at her first large law firm:

> "Everyone makes mistakes, but if you aren't working for people who are going to mentor you and be interested in your forward progression and professional development, then your mistakes are going to be seen differently. You're not going to be able to have space to make mistakes. You can still be successful, but it'll be harder."

Regardless of all these warnings, if you're like me, these caution signals seem like they may not apply to you.

You've worked hard. You've done your research. You know that as an under-represented minority, if you go to a top fourteen school, your odds of earning a $190,000 salary greatly increase. If you've already interned at a few law firms and have an idea that you could like the work, you *know* it'll be possible to pay down your law school loans in the future.

But the question still remains, "Is going down this arduous route going to provide me a with a substantially more secure living than going down another path would?"

According to Aubrey, the answer is absolutely and fundamentally, "No."

> "A law degree isn't a guarantee for financial stability, at least it's not what it used to be. You shouldn't do law school unless you really want to practice. If you really want to practice, you should get a kick-ass LSAT score and get good grades. Each school's rankings will tell you the percentage of people who have a job a year after graduating. I'd look at those. If you think you know what you want to do after law school, look at where those people went to school. You have to hold on to every advantage that you have in order to be successful in the law."

Aubrey demonstrated the importance of using these advantages by highlighting an individual who graduated from a top ten Ivy League law program—University of Pennsylvania Law—and has struggled with employment ever since:

> "There was a gentleman that was at the law firm as a summer associate, and he was very... haughty. I interviewed him for the summer program. I remember seeing his transcript from UPenn and he had not done especially well. But he felt like since he went to UPenn he could do whatever he wanted and was going to get a job. He's not at a large firm now and has jumped from firm to firm."

Here's the bottom line.

There are a lot of benefits of attending a top law school. It confers a level of prestige, teaches you how to think, and can help you expand your network. However, as we have learned, these benefits are also available from other professions such as consulting and human resources. If you want the long-term stability associated with going to law school, you're going to need amazing test scores, ideally a degree from a top fourteen program, three years of extremely diligent work that places you at the top 25 percent of your class, and a strong interest in and aptitude for legal practice that can sustain for the length of your career.

If that's the path you'd like to take, there's nothing wrong with that. I personally enjoyed a lot of my time in the legal field, so if law interests you, you should absolutely not let other people's fears sway you from pursuing it.

But as we have learned so far, there are other paths to success available. Let's find out how to pursue them and whether or not you should.

11

DO YOU REALLY WANT TO PURSUE YOUR DREAM?

If you picked up this book, there's a good chance you have thought about pursuing a dream. In America, the urge to pursue your dreams is nearly embedded into the fabric of the country. The United States has always been a place to which immigrants come to pursue their dreams; they leave their homes for the opportunity of a better life. As a result, the country is largely filled with those who believe that following a dream, despite the risk, is the best move to make.

American culture glorifies dream pursuit and risk-taking. In fact, there's an entire economy built around taking advantage of this feature of western culture: advertising. Americans receive constant messaging from advertisers, life coaches, and motivational speakers that if they don't take a risk and pursue their dreams (read: buy their product), they'll regret their decision and be immensely unhappy.

During my quarter-life crisis before law school, I bought into this messaging heavily. It felt like my world was falling apart, so I tried to build more discipline in my life to give me some semblance of stability. As most people do in these situations, I turned to Google. I watched countless videos about how to "master the day" and "reach your full potential." I watched Eric Thomas yell at school-aged kids about how they should need to succeed as bad as they want to breathe.[111] I listened to advice compilations from successful people; the one piece of advice that stood out to me most was Jeff Bezos saying that he left his highly lucrative job to start Amazon because he knew he would regret not trying for the rest of his life.[112]

The intended effect of all this stuff is clear: inspire the audience by positioning the chase for one's dreams as not only a worthy pursuit, but also as an escape hatch from a less than ideal life. For someone who feels down on their luck, stuck in a rut, or fearful that they might be missing out, suggestions like this can be quite captivating, and in some cases can even inspire (often inadvisable) action.

Especially when you consider that this type of content is frequently paired with images of fame, luxury, photoshopped bodies, and an overall veneer that screams, "You can confidently expect have this level of success if you take a risk, work hard, and buy my course/shoe/book."

---

111 Eric Thomas, "Secrets to success Pt. 1," Etthehiphoppreacher, December 11, 2008, YouTube video, 9:01.

112 *Evan Carmichael*, "No regrets - Jeff Bezos - Have NO regrets," June 15, 2014, YouTube video, 2:59.

Some people champion following your dreams for attention, some people do it with a genuine intent to inspire, and some people encourage you so that you'll purchase their course or coaching services. Some want all three. None of that's a problem.

What *is* a problem, however, is that it's unclear how valuable it is to chase your dreams in terms of one's overall life satisfaction. This uncertainty is what drives the dilemma that many children of immigrants face. We've been raised on the family ethos of "work hard and become a doctor, lawyer, or engineer" and while we may have some (or a lot of) reservations, it appears to be a straight shot to a reasonable level of success. Nevertheless, we often also feel like we may be missing out on the American Dream by not following our own passions and desires.

The problem of course is that while being a famous actor or rapper would be great, many of us don't really know how to make that happen, and if we fail, our parents might legitimately die from social embarrassment. Plus, when we're really honest about it, there's a not-so-small part of us that wants what our parents want. We could make them happy (and less stressed) by carving out a stable life as a doctor, lawyer, or engineer.

This is the dilemma that I faced. What is it really that I want? Is leaving law school to become an entrepreneur going to bring me fulfillment or is it just going to shred my confidence, embarrass my family, and leave me hollowed out on the side of the road? Is going to law school going to bring me the stability and prestige that my parents desire or is it just going to shred my dreams, burn me out, and leave me with a possible alcohol addiction after a few years?

According to Mark Manson, author of the New York Times Best Seller *The Subtle Art of Not Giving a F*ck*, the answers to my questions are a bit more nuanced than one might expect. Manson points out that while we can never be certain if we're better off not pursuing our dreams, there are two guidelines that can help:

FALL IN LOVE WITH THE PROCESS, NOT THE RESULT.

According to Manson, the fallacy that many of us make when deciding on a career is believing that a path we currently don't enjoy will magically become better after we hit a particular milestone or obtain a particular position.[113]

For example, many law students graduate law school and begin working seventy- to eighty-hour weeks under high-stress deadlines, doing work that doesn't necessarily fulfill them.[114]

According to an often-cited Johns Hopkins University study of more than one hundred occupations, researchers found that lawyers lead the nation with the highest incidence of depression. The American Bar Association estimates that

113 Mark Manson, "Why Some Dreams Should Not Be Pursued," *Mark Manson - Life Advice That Doesn't Suck*, accessed September 16, 2020.

114 Sally Kane, "The Realities and Myths of Practicing Law," The Balance Careers, last modified October 7, 2019.

15 to 20 percent of all US lawyers suffer from alcoholism or substance abuse.[115]

Nevertheless, many persist in the field of law with the expectation that they'll make partner or rise up high enough to alleviate their suffering. But as Sarah Cottrell, founder of the Former Lawyer Collaborative, points out: "that is a never-ending treadmill." Further even if this stress-alleviating position exists, it will be extremely challenging to get, and if you don't make it there you can reasonably "expect to spend well over 60 hours a week (not including weekends) being at the beck and call of the managing partners."[116]

Again, not everyone has this relationship with the law. There are thousands of lawyers who love practicing and would not want to do anything else. But according to Manson, our society's fixation on results drives 70 percent of us into the wrong pursuits and career paths. However, by focusing on the process and by paying attention to whether or not we enjoy it, we can drastically improve our odds of success.[117]

WHAT'S MOTIVATING YOU?

According to Manson, the answers to whether you should pursue our dream or stick with your present path can also

---

115 Tyger Latham, "The Depressed Lawyer," *Psychology Today*, May 2, 2011.

116 Ibid.

117 Mark Manson, "Why Some Dreams Should Not Be Pursued," *Mark Manson - Life Advice That Doesn't Suck*, accessed September 16, 2020.

be found by taking a really hard look at what's motivating your interest in your dream.[118]

Sometimes our desires can cover up painful emotions or traumas that we're unaware of or unwilling to simply sit with. If that sounds crazy, just think about someone eating a gallon of ice cream and binge-watching Netflix as they overcome a breakup. They aren't really passionate about ice cream or reality TV—they just serve as a welcome distraction from the underlying pain that they're feeling. The same thing can happen with our interests and career choices.

But other times, our desires come out of a genuine expression of enthusiasm and joy. We absolutely love what we're doing and want to do it all the time. In those instances, the notion of pursuing your dreams is much more realistic. When the going gets tough, and things aren't working out exactly as you had hoped, you will be more likely to push through until you achieve your goal.

Manson explains how this phenomenon manifested in his own life:

> "For most of my adolescence and young adulthood, I fantasized about being a musician—a rock star, in particular. Any badass guitar song I heard, I would always close my eyes and envision myself up on stage playing it to the screams of the crowd, people absolutely losing their minds to my sweet finger-noodling. This fantasy could keep me occupied for hours on end.

118 Ibid.

> “The fantasizing continued up through college, even after I dropped out of music school and stopped playing seriously. But even then it was never a question of if I’d ever be up playing in front of screaming crowds, but when. I was biding my time until I could invest the effort into getting out there and making it work.

But despite fantasizing for over half of his life, Manson’s dream never came true. His reasoning: he didn’t actually want it.

> “I’m in love with the result—the image of me on stage, people cheering, me rocking out, putting everything I have into what I’m playing—but I’m not in love with the process.” continued Manson

Manson realized that the more mundane, and routine aspects of becoming a “rock star,” like rehearsing, finding gigs, getting people to show up, and so forth, were not interesting to him at all. It was imagining being on stage in front of thousands of screaming fans, that he really enjoyed.

> “It’s a mountain of a dream and a mile-high climb to the top. And what it took me a long time to discover is that I don’t like to climb, I just want to imagine the top.”
>
> MARK MANSON, AUTHOR OF *THE SUBTLE ART OF NOT GIVING A F*CK*

"Our culture would tell me that I've somehow failed myself. Self-help would say that I either wasn't courageous enough, determined enough, or I didn't believe in myself enough. Lifestyle designers would tell me that I gave in to my conventional role in society. I'd be told to do affirmations or join a mastermind group or something.

"But the truth is far less interesting than that: I thought I wanted something. But I didn't. End of story.

"I've since discovered that the rock star fantasy has less to do with actually rocking out on stage than simply feeling acknowledged and appreciated. It's no coincidence that as my personal relationships improve dramatically, the fantasy slowly fades into the background. It's a periodic mental indulgence now, not a driving need."[119]

Manson's realization is one with which many of us can not only resonate, but it's also backed up by science. Researchers Paul O'Keefe, Carol Dweck, and Gregory Walton sought to answer the question of whether or not one should actually seek to "find their passion."

"People are often told to find their passion as though passions and interests are pre-formed and must simply be discovered," say the researchers.[120]

---

119 Manson, "Why Some Dreams Should Not Be Pursued."

120 Paul A. O'Keefe, Carol S. Dweck, Gregory M. Walton, "Implicit Theories of Interest: Finding Your Passion or Developing It?," *Psychological Science* 29, no. 10 (September 2018): 1653-1664.

According to the data they collected during their study, this belief is not only flawed, but it's also potentially detrimental to the actual development of one's passions. "The message to find your passion is generally offered with good intentions, to convey: *Do not worry so much about talent, do not bow to pressure for status or money, just find what is meaningful and interesting to you.* Unfortunately, the belief system this message may engender can undermine the very development of people's interests."[121]

Specifically, their research showed that when people believe that passions are found—otherwise known as "fixed theory"—it's "more likely to dampen interest in areas outside people's existing interests." Additionally, "those endorsing a fixed theory were also more likely to anticipate boundless motivation when passions were found, not anticipating possible difficulties." Moreover, when engaging in a new interest became difficult, study participants demonstrated a marked decrease in their desire to continue with the relevant interest.[122]

I think many of us are familiar with this phenomenon. You "find" a new diet that seems perfect. It seems like it's going to solve your weight issues once and for all. It's aligned with your beliefs about food. It seems simple. And like with most things, it goes well at first, confirming that your suspicions were right. You've found the perfect diet. Right?

Wrong.

---

121 Ibid.

122 Ibid.

Out of nowhere, you hit a few roadblocks. Trying to stay away from bread during outings with friends is more difficult than you imagined. You're "eating right" but you're no longer losing any weight. Your new diet-friendly grocery bill is higher than you had expected. And in a matter of weeks, this once perfect diet is no longer perfect. It's no longer the clear path to success that you imagined. So, you drop it, claiming, it just wasn't right for you.

The underlying, misguided assumption in that scenario is that the "right" diet won't be difficult. It won't be filled with obstacles, or pain, or suffering. But this couldn't be further from the truth. O'Keefe and his research team use another analogy explain the idea more clearly: love.

> "People can believe that successful relationships are destined or cultivated. . . people see dating as an attempt to find 'the one.' Faced with relationship challenges, people may quickly move on. However, if someone views love and dating as something challenging yet rewarding and something that doesn't have to be perfect, that "can increase people's motivation to maintain relationships and resolve differences when they arise (Knee, 1988; Knee et al., 2002)."[123]

Let's apply this analogy to our passions and interests. If you believe that you're searching for "the one"—your one true passion—you're likely to move on from that passion when things get difficult. If, however, you believe that your interests and passions must be cultivated in order for them to thrive

123 O'Keefe et. al., "Implicit Theories of Interest."

and you expect some roadblocks along the way, you're likely to not give up at the first signs of difficulty.

If we return to Manson's rock star dream, we can see that he was operating under the assumption that once he was able to "dive in," everything would work out and he would be a rock star in no time. Once he realized that he would have to cultivate his interest, doing the routine and often times mundane tasks necessary reach his idyllic Rockstar image, his drive dropped substantially.[124]

As I also learned the hard way, pursuing your dream is not a guarantee of success, only a guarantee that you're pursuing your dream. Making your dreams come true is most likely to occur when you cultivate them gradually, and such cultivation usually does not require a dramatic shift in another direction.

So, for those of you who picked up this book because you're certain you want to pursue a dream, it may be useful to first consider these questions:

- Do you fantasize more about the end result than you do the process?
- If your goal is to pursue a dream, what do you think will happen when you pursue it? Why do you believe those things will happen?
- Are there ways that you can cultivate your "dream" on your current path without going out to "find" it?

---

124 Manson, "Why Some Dreams Should Not Be Pursued."

While disregarding your current, secure path for the sake of "finding your passion" may work out for you, you may want to instead think about how you can cultivate your passion where you are and what circumstances are necessary for you to do so. We'll discuss how to do this in the following chapters.

12

THE IMPORTANCE OF HAVING A PLAN

Hopefully by this stage in the book, you have a slightly better idea of your situation.

Perhaps you've decided that you're actually passionate about law, medicine, or engineering, or that you're going to work on cultivating your dream in your down time.

Perhaps you've realized that law, medicine, and engineering are truly *not* for you and that you're ready to make a complete switch to your dream career.

Or perhaps you still have no idea what you want to do but you definitely don't want to take on $200,000 in debt to figure out what the answer is.

Regardless of your situation, there's one thing that will make this whole process a lot less painful for both you and your parents: a plan.

According to Merriam Webster, a plan is "a method to achieving an end."[125] Needless to say, some methods are better than others, and your ability to accurately and succinctly explain it will play a large role in your ability to get buy-in, not only from your parents but also from yourself.

As we discussed in the first part of this book, first-generation parents generally have a strong prevention focus. They've already taken a chance by coming to the United States, and now their goal is to maximize the return on their investment. As such, they are looking for opportunities with a clear path to success with which they are familiar enough to provide some insight or guidance to help steer you in the right direction. Law, medicine, and engineering all fall into that category.

As a result, revealing your idea to stray from the beaten path will fill your parents with heart-racing anxiety and nervousness. According to Rachel Botsman, author of *Who Can You Trust* and a Trust Fellow at the University of Oxford's Saïd School of Business, the reason for parents' anxiety really comes down to trust.

As Botsman points out in her new LinkedIn series "Rethink," a trust state is "a person's tolerance to risk and uncertainty with a specific situation."[126] If you're in a high trust state, you can cope with unknowns such as:

- Not knowing the end goal or outcome.

---

125 *Merriam-Webster*, s.v. "plan (*n.*)," accessed October 5, 2020.

126 Rachel Botsman, "I Don't Know What to Say," LinkedIn, published June 15, 2020.

- Not knowing the timeframe around something.
- Not knowing what might happen next.
- Not having the full picture.

Unless you're following the path of becoming a doctor, lawyer, or engineer, your parent's trust state around any other career path is likely quite low. And while your parents' expression of their distrust likely isn't personal, it's still quite hard to not take it personally. For someone who's spent their entire life seeking the approval and encouragement of their parents, realizing that they don't trust you to navigate a new, unknown scenario on your own can be destabilizing. However, there is a way to regain that stability: create a plan.

Botsman provides a colorful example of why plans are important tools for managing people with low trust states:

> "The events I would normally do in front of a live audience have moved into virtual formats. Whilst I deeply miss the human connection of being on a stage with people in the room, I'm finding it creatively rewarding to design virtual experiences. My clients don't always feel the same. They are nervous. I was starting to feel a bit frustrated about how many calls, check-ins and ultimately, how much visibility they wanted into the process. When you get on stage, nobody knows what will happen! Indeed, the magic of public speaking comes from letting go. And then I realised something powerful: **people don't know what to expect.**"[127]

---

127 Botsman, "I Don't Know What to Say."

Your parents, like Botsman's clients, are nervous. Although you're extremely excited about this new journey that you want to embark on, your parents likely don't feel the same. They're comfortable with the way things are. Unlike you, they don't have deep knowledge of your abilities and motivation, nor do they know how you plan to go about making this dream a reality.

According to Botsman, we can remedy uncertainty by doing three things:

- Creating clarity and purpose
- Setting clear expectations
- Giving people control

By satisfying these in your plan, you'll be on the right path to not only improve your parents' trust state, but you'll also greatly increase your likelihood of following through with the successful cultivation of your dream.

CREATING CLARITY AND PURPOSE

The first thing you need to do when crafting a plan is create clarity and purpose.

The truth is, if you're going into medicine, law, or engineering, there's plenty of clarity and obvious purpose. The purpose of going into medical school, for example, is clearly to become a doctor. The method for achieving this goal is also clear: complete the required years of school, score high on your exams, and you'll become a doctor.

If your goal is to go into another less traditional area of interest, you'll need to make greater efforts to communicate the purpose of pursuing this field and provide ample clarity about how you'll make it happen.

For example, when I approached my parents about deferring my entrance into law school, I said I wanted to "explore my interests in entrepreneurship." When they understandably pushed back, their first questions were, "Why?" (read: purpose) and "How?" (read: clarity). They wanted to know why I was suddenly no longer gung ho about law school and what pursuing entrepreneurship would accomplish. My answer was underwhelming to say the least. They then inquired about how I would make this endeavor happen. With an undeserved level of confidence, I explained that I planned to live with them while applying to "entrepreneurial" jobs. When I landed one, I would be off to the races. This explanation, of course, didn't clarify anything for my parents.

In hindsight, my purpose was to pursue my dream while it was still an economically and socially viable thing to do. I didn't have a six-figure salary to walk away from, and at twenty-five, I was still young enough for future employers to consider my journey as endearing and inspiring. I could have clarified how I would pursue my dream by working with my alumni career counselor to put together a short timeline for my deferral and a list of companies to which I would apply.

By creating clarity and purpose, you'll be able to mitigate many of your parents' concerns and also set yourself up for success as you begin your journey. You don't need an overly specific plan—in fact, over-planning might stop you from ever beginning. But having even a simple plan will instill in you the necessary confidence to push through to success.

SET CLEAR EXPECTATIONS

The next thing that you need to focus on is setting clear expectations.

One of the benefits of medicine, law, and engineering is the crystal-clear expectations. There's no uncertainty for you or your parents about what they can expect by you entering one of these fields.

When it comes to other fields, such as comedy, for example, the expectations are much less clear. An article in the *Hollywood Reporter* recently (and falsely) claimed that a "newer comic just breaking into the L.A. circuit can earn anywhere from $1,250 to $2,500 per week."[128]

This figure works out to roughly $120,000 a year. As you can imagine, veteran comedians vehemently refuted this claim.

> As comedian Moses Storm put it: "I'm eight years into comedy. Started in L.A. with a few TV credits and a late-night set and was not even close to earning [the] amount [cited in the article]. Not only have I never made that amount, it's very hard to make that amount even on the road, and that's probably the only place

128 Justin Caffier, "Comedians Reveal What the L.A. Stand-up Scene Actually Pays," Vulture, accessed October 9, 2020.

you *can* make money. On a very good week, where you get to do the rare few shows that do pay in L.A., you're making maybe $51.

"So to paint a picture that live comedy pays, which is quite literally what this article says, is irresponsible. I don't know many teens in Iowa that are reading *The Hollywood Reporter*, but if they are, they're gonna be like me at eighteen and trying to add up the numbers, like, *Can I survive and sustain myself doing this?* To mislead someone with a figure that is beyond an exaggeration and just ridiculous—if you're making $2,500 a week, that's $10,000 a month? That's $120,000 a year?!—it's irresponsible. Anyone looking to move out to L.A. is desperate for any piece of information that can make them feel better or sway their opinion, and this potential six-figure income now out there? It's insane. I don't even know what to say."[129]

Due to the presence of misinformation like the article from the *Hollywood Reporter,* it's essential to do your research about what you can reasonably expect from your journey. Your parents should be fully aware of the inherent risks and how you're planning to feed, house, and clothe yourself, especially if it involves a stipend from them. If you don't have the answers to these questions, take your time and try to figure it out. If your plan involves them, either financially or otherwise, show them the specific way that they can support you during this time. Don't spring this plan on them and expect them to simply be ready to support you no matter your goal.

---

129 Caffier, "Comedians Reveal What the L.A. Stand-up Scene Actually Pays."

GIVE PEOPLE CONTROL

Lastly, you want your parents to have some control. The truth of the matter is, whether you like it or not, your parents are accustomed to having a controlling interest in the way your life unfolds.

Think about the way you feel when you're in the car with someone for the first time. Unless they drive like a driving instructor, you'll likely experience a few anxiety-producing moments. The reason for your anxiety is that you aren't in control. You've driven a car before, so you know that you would've pressed the brake sooner when that car ahead of you slowed down. You know the *exact* distance you should keep between you and the other cars when changing lanes. So, if you are in the passenger's seat with this new person driving, you're understandably going to be panicked.

You can minimize a lot of your parent's fear, however, by giving them some control. The best way to do so is to include them in the development of some of your plans. Create a few different options for how you want to go about pursuing your dream and ask your parents for help in refining them. Even if you end up going an entirely different route, research shows that letting them feel like they had some say over your plan will comfort them.[130]

If you're doubtful of this step's importance, think about how many crosswalk buttons are simply mechanical placebos to help us be more patient while waiting for the signal to change;

---

130 Jacopo Prisco, "Illusion of Control: Why the World Is Full of Buttons that Don't Work," CNN, accessed October 9, 2020.

> "'They're sometimes called 'placebo buttons'—buttons that are mechanically sound and can be pushed, but provide no functionality. Like placebo pills, however, these buttons may still serve a purpose,' according to Ellen Langer, a Harvard psychologist who pioneered a concept known as the 'illusion of control.' 'They do have a psychological effect,' she said in a phone interview. 'Taking some action leads people to feel a sense of control over a situation, and that feels good, rather than just being a passive bystander. Doing something typically feels better than doing nothing.'"[131]

By implementing these approaches prior to beginning your journey, you'll not only better preserve your parents' mental health but also improve your chances of executing your plan properly, which we will discuss next.

KEY TAKEAWAYS

- Depending on how far off the beaten path you intend to go, your parents will likely have a low trust state around your ability to achieve your goal.
- You can increase your parents' trust state by creating a thorough plan.
- By co-creating your plan alongside your parents and giving them the feeling of control, you can reduce some of their stress and increase your likelihood of success.

---

131 Ibid.

13

HOW TO CHOOSE THE RIGHT PLAN

Developing a plan is definitely a great way to reduce everyone's anxiety and maximize your likelihood of success. However, the difficulty tends to arise when it comes down to deciding what is the right plan for *you*.

I remember feeling this way while trying to decide whether or not I should take a leave of absence from law school. I think I spent more time talking to people and thinking about what I should do than actually attending class. In retrospect, what I wanted—in true perfectionist fashion—was for someone to give me an answer that would be the unambiguously correct choice to make. So, I talked to entrepreneurs and lawyers. I read blog posts and watched videos. I walked aimlessly through New York City, noodling through all the conflicting advice I had received in hopes that I could figure out the best decision. And after all that, I still ended up taking a death-defying leap from law school with no plan to support myself.

I knew I would always be able to find an excuse not to leave. I knew myself. I knew there would never be a right time, and that if I didn't leap at that moment, I never would. So, I jumped. In reality, after I did, I felt instant regret. I even sent an email to the dean of students at the law school to see if I could change my mind. Once the adrenaline had worn off, I fell into a deep depression for a few weeks. My back-of-the-envelope plan was in shreds and I had to move back home with my parents. While I now look back on the period with fondness, it wasn't very pleasant at the time.

Interestingly, many reading this book will see my story and the stories of my interviewees and come to the conclusion that they should do also make the jump; if I did it without a plan, it'll work out for them as well. That's not necessarily the case. My path is different from anyone else's, and a whole host of circumstances made my particular journey end on a good note rather than a bad one.

There are so many paths to "success." As Stanford professors Bill Burnett and Dave Evans argue in their book *Designing Your Life*, the notion that there's one optimal path to take is a dysfunctional belief.[132] You may see several possible ways to go about achieving your goal. Your friends, family, and acquaintances will likely give their own unsolicited advice, too. They might even call your plan ridiculous. But it's not because they're mean or insensitive. It's simply because when so many paths to different types of success exist, everyone has a different perspective.

---

132 Bill Burnett and Dave Evans, *Designing Your Life: How to Build A Well-Lived, Joyful Life* (New York: Alfred A. Knopf, 2016), 87.

Consider the debacle around the color-changing dress that overtook the internet in 2015. While the dress was actually blue and black, many people who saw the image thought it looked white and gold instead.[133] This same phenomenon takes place when it comes to your life. Many will see what you present and feel you should *obviously* go in one direction while others will say that you should *obviously* go the opposite way.

Asking as many people as possible and choosing the path with the most votes is one way to make your decision, but that's not always the best way to settle on an option that works for you. Another approach which may lead you to more ideal outcomes is to focus less on getting advice from others and more on making decisions that feel satisfying to *you*.

Stephen Ozoigbo, a first-generation Nigerian and venture capitalist, put it this way during our interview: "One of the key things I've learned is that life as we know it now is moving away from standardization and moving towards personalization... the notion of, 'Do it this way because it's this way' is no longer feasible." As Stephen suggests, reaching ideal outcomes isn't about following someone else's prescribed steps to success. The world is evolving too quickly to rely such an outdated method. You need to internally examine your skills and interests and take an approach that works for you in your unique circumstances.

One of the best ways to figure out what works best for you is to design what Bill Burnett and Dave Evans call "Odyssey

---

133 Brad Plumer, "The Science Behind that Absurd Color-Changing dress, Explained," Vox, published February 27, 2015.

Plans": three different versions of the next five years of your life, written on a sheet of paper. The goal of such a plan isn't to rank them but rather to determine three possible plans that each reflect you, your skills, and your interests.[134]

Your first plan should center around either the extended version of life that you're currently living or the amazing idea that you've been holding onto for some time. It's the idea you already have—a good idea that deserves substantive attention.[135]

Your second plan should center around what you'd do if you suddenly could no longer do your first plan. For example, your first plan was to start your own line of hard seltzers but the FDA suddenly announces that seltzers cause cancer. What would you do in this situation? What would you pursue if the first plan is no longer a viable option?[136]

The third plan should focus on what you'd do if money or image were no object. If you knew you could make a decent living and no one would think less of you for doing it, what would you do? The plan may not actually be feasible but writing it down can really help clarify whether or not the next step feels right for you.

After doing this exercise for myself, I realized that I could be very happy with not returning to law school but that I could also be happy in a scenario where I *did* go back and finish.

---

134 Burnett and Evans, *Designing Your Life.*

135 Ibid.

136 Ibid.

Discovering this alleviated most of my stress and made the decision feel less like life or death. Doing this exercise also helped my parents see the long-term view for my other career options, reducing their fears as well. If you actually do this exercise and don't overthink it, you can actually change your life.[137]

If you'd like help building the right plan for you, you can schedule a time to chat with me at https://www.noodle.consulting.

137 Burnett and Evans, *Designing Your Life.*

CONCLUSION

It's my hope that you now have a better idea of how to build your dreams without giving your parents a heart attack.

We've discussed how your parents are a lot like investors and how they want to help ensure their investment is successful.

We've examined how law, medicine, and engineering are historically regarded as good fields to enter to achieve stable success. We've also discovered that this security only exists if you're motivated to not only complete the requisite education but to also maintain the demanding lifestyle that these professions often require.

We've also learned about other available professions that are less arduous and can also provide a high quality of life.

We've explored why immigrant cultures place less emphasis on individuality than western culture does and how this difference impacts decision-making for children of immigrants.

Finally, we've gone over the importance of having a plan and how to co-create one alongside your parents that's unique to you and your circumstances. I discussed all of this in the hope that you can increase your odds of success in whatever path you choose and minimize the amount of stress that your parents experience along your journey.

Unfortunately, as I discovered, despite everything discussed in this book, you might still be unsure about the best approach to your future and, if you're anything like me, you might have constant, low-level anxiety about what will happen next in your life. You may, like me, end up making a hard left without a real plan. You may decide to place your dream on the back burner for the next few years. You may develop a thriving side business while completing medical school. We can't predict the future or what will end up being the best decision in the long run.

So, here is my suggestion. If you take away nothing else from this book, ask yourself these three questions inspired by Dr. Robert Pearl, a professor at the Stanford Graduate Schools of Business and Medicine:

- What's the worst thing that could happen?
- How would my parents feel if that outcome occurred?
- How would I feel if that outcome occurred?

These questions are designed to help counteract the phenomenon called "brainshift," a subconscious neuro-biological sequence that can cause us to perceive the world around us "in ways that contradict objective reality, distorting what we see and hear."[138] Brainshift tends to happen in situations that involve high anxiety or major reward, like when trying to decide whether or not to pursue a dream.

If you ask yourself these questions before you act and visualize yourself in each scenario, you'll likely make a decision with which both you and your parents can live and thrive.

No heart attacks needed.

---

138 Robert Pearl, "The Science of Regrettable Decisions," Vox, published July 23, 2019.

ACKNOWLEDGEMENTS

I want to express my deepest gratitude to the people who preordered this book. Having each of you in my corner made all the difference in bringing this book to life.

Sarah Cottrell
Neil Irvin
Denise Nwaezeapu
Jessica Woolley
Sonia Montenegro
Vida Anderson
Aisha S. Greene
Diarra McKinney
Claudia Alarco Alarco
Thomas Mehari
Ryan Compton
Vivek Ramakrishnan
Maria Guevara
Justin Mayes
Nana Abrefah
Yvonne Kamdem
Ximena Morales
Tayonna Ngutter
Temitope Tuby-Lukan
Eric Wilson
Alicia Cortez
Henry Hawkins
Niki Chinamanthur
Joe Gomez
Jacque W. Leighty
Sarah Iyere
Max Payton
Aniekeme Umoh
Kenneth Horenstein
Shaneisha Wofford
Jerry Fox
Andrea Boutros
Kwame Boler
Deborah Owolabi
Dawn Jefferson
Marsha Chinician
Hattie Shaw
Ingrid Campbell
Lewshá Washington
Melinda Han
Jeremy Meyers
Sahir Raoof

Chris Wallace
Amana Bawa
Lizette Morin
Danah Screen
Karin Tolgu
Michael Luciani
Eric Koester
Ashley Joyce
Joshua Foster
Josh Bush
Christina Cyr
Ade Sawyer
Dominic Edwards
Jameil Brown
Chelsa Thompson
Caleb Woods
Eric Coly
Sheldon Novek
Ashley Nemeth
Deborah Finch
Monifa Hall
Fatimatou Diallo
Grey Lane
Lizette Morin
Lee Negroni
Eddie Kim
Josh Bush
Othanya Garcia
Kodjo Kumi
Shelby Horner
Nick Ellingson
Cameron Fegers
Lauren Lockett
Erica Dsouza
Adrian Silver
Hilary Higgins
Adam Bresgi
Erica Brackett
Aazim Jafarey
Uche Iteogu
Kelly Carde
Pradyumna Modukuru
Ruth Fikeru
Myles Granatham
Claire Lee
Kirby Winfield
Jolanda Lippold
Chike Nwaezeapu
Naomi Dubisette
Joseph Kemp
Abbie Lewis
Sunny Singh

APPENDIX

INTRODUCTION

Columbia Law School. "Employment Statistics." Accessed August 28, 2020. https://www.law.columbia.edu/careers/employment-statistics.

Sloan, Karen. "Want to Work in Big Law? These Schools Are Good Bets." Law.com. Published March 5, 2020. https://www.law.com/2020/03/05/want-to-work-in-big-law-these-schools-are-good-bets/?slreturn=20200921144234

Thoreau, Henry David. *Walden*. New York: Thomas Y. Crowell & Company, 1910.

U.S. News & World Report. "2021 Best Law Schools." Accessed October 21, 2020. https://www.usnews.com/best-graduate-schools/top-law-schools/law-rankings

CHAPTER 1

Buhr, Sarah. "Yo Raises $1.5M In Funding at a $10M Valuation, Investors Include Betaworks and Pete Cashmore." TechCrunch. Published July 18, 2014. https://techcrunch.com/2014/07/18/yo-raises-1-5m-in-funding-at-a-10m-valuation-investors-include-betaworks-and-pete-cashmore/.

Grant, Heidi. "The Hidden Danger of Being Risk-Averse." *Harvard Business Review,* July 2, 2013. https://hbr.org/2013/07/hidden-danger-of-being-risk-averse.

Investopedia, s.v. "Angel Investor," updated July 26, 2020. https://www.investopedia.com/terms/a/angelinvestor.asp.

Investopedia. s.v. "Term Sheet." Updated March 19, 2020. https://www.investopedia.com/terms/t/termsheet.asp.

Kruppa, Miles. "For Silicon Valley Tech Tycoons, Angel Investing is a Status Symbol." *Los Angeles Times.* February 25, 2020. Business. https://www.latimes.com/business/story/2020-02-25/tech-tycoons-angel-investing.

CHAPTER 2

American Academy of Neurology. "How to Become a Neurologist." Accessed August 28, 2020. https://www.aan.com/tools-and-resources/medical-students/careers-in-neurology/how-to-become-a-neurologist/.

CDL.com. "Becoming a CDL Driver." Accessed August 28, 2020. https://www.cdl.com/becoming-a-cdl-driver.

PRNewswire. "Doctors without Jobs Says Recent Residency Match Leaves More U.S. Physicians Jobless." Business Insider. Published April 22, 2019. https://markets.businessinsider.com/news/stocks/doctors-without-jobs-says-recent-residency-match-leaves-more-u-s-physicians-jobless-1028126544.

U.S. Bureau of Labor Statistics. "Occupational Employment and Wages, May 2019, 53-3032 Heavy and Tractor-Trailer Truck Drivers." Last modified July 6, 2020. https://www.bls.gov/oes/current/oes533032.htm.

CHAPTER 3

Advantour. "Teacher's Day - Festive Date in China." Accessed September 5, 2020. https://www.advantour.com/china/holidays/teachers.

Chua, Amy. *Battle Hymn of The Tiger Mother.* New York: The Penguin Press, 2010.

Curran, Thomas and Andrew P. Hill. "Perfectionism Is Increasing over Time: A Meta-Analysis of Birth Cohort Differences from 1989 to 2016." *American Psychological Association - Psychological Bulletin 145, no. 4,* (2019): 410-429. https://doi.org/10.1037/bul0000138.

Dahl, Melissa. "Comparison is the thief of joy, so why can't we stop?" CNN Health. Accessed September 5, 2020. https://www.cnn.com/2015/10/27/health/comparing-yourself-with-peers/index.html.

Dale, Stacy and Alan B. Krueger. "Estimating the Return to College Selectivity over the Career Using Administrative Earnings Data." Journal of Human Resources 49, no. 2 (Spring 2014): 323-358. https://www.doi.org/ 10.3386/w17159.

Encyclopaedia Britannica Online, Academic ed. s.v. "Confucius." Accessed September 5, 2020. https://www.britannica.com/biography/Confucius.

Forbes. "ForbesQuotes: Thoughts on The Business of Life." Accessed September 5, 2020. https://www.forbes.com/quotes/8988/.

Kelly, James. "Maslow's Hierarchy of Needs." The Peak Performance Center. Accessed October 8, 2020. https://thepeakperformancecenter.com/educational-learning/learning/principles-of-learning/maslows-hierarchy-needs/.

Kim, Su Yeong. "Defining Tiger Parenting in Chinese Americans." *Human Development* 56, no. 4 (September 2013): 217–222. https://dx.doi.org/10.1159%2F000353711.

Liu, Cha-Hsuan. TEDx Talks. "The Secret of Tiger Moms." Published June 14, 2017. YouTube Video, 13:35. https://youtube.com/watch?v=JgAJkpclV9M.

"LSAT Scores: the Good, the Bad & the Average." Chegg. Accessed September 5, 2020. https://www.chegg.com/test-prep-blog/lsat/lsat-scores-the-good-the-bad-the-average/.

Marissa. "Why Your GPA Matters." *College Dreams* (blog). *The California State University.* Accessed October 8, 2020. https://blogs.calstate.edu/college/why-your-gpa-matters/.

McLeod, Saul. "Maslow's Hierarchy of Needs." SimplyPsychology. Last updated March 20, 2020. https://www.simplypsychology.org/maslow.html.

Merriam-Webster. s.v. "self-actualize (v.)." Accessed September 4, 2020. https://www.merriam-webster.com/dictionary/self-actualize.

Porter, Eduardo. "A Simple Equation: More Education = More Income." *New York Times.* Published September 10, 2014. https://www.nytimes.com/2014/09/11/business/economy/a-simple-equation-more-education-more-income.html.

Vault Guide to the Top 100 Law Firms, 2018 Edition. s.v. "Cooley LLP." Vault. Accessed October 8, 2020. https://www.cooley.com/-/media/cooley/pdf/reprints/2017/2018-vault-profile.ashx?la=en&hash=BD85461992E8C03B0C19E675CAA76717.

CHAPTER 4

Casimir, Leslie. "Data Show Nigerians the Most Educated in the U.S." *Houston Chronicle.* Last modified January 12, 2018. https://www.chron.com/news/article/Data-show-Nigerians-the-most-educated-in-the-U-S-1600808.php.

Flett, Gordon, Paul Hewitt, Joan Oliver, and Silvana Macdonald. *Perfectionism: Theory, Research, and Treatment.* Washington, DC: American Psychological Association, 2002.

Lewis, Sam. "Why VPs Should Care About Engineer Burnout." *PagerDuty Blog.* PagerDuty, September 8, 2015. https://www.pagerduty.com/blog/why-vps-should-care-engineer-burnout/.

Mangan, Kate. "How to Recognize and Prevent Lawyer Burnout." Lawyerist. Last updated August 1, 2019. https://lawyerist.com/blog/recognize-prevent-lawyer-burnout/.

Oxford Research Encyclopedia, Psychology. s.v. "Perfectionism and Performance in Sport, Education, and the Workplace." Accessed October 8, 2020. https://oxfordre.com/psychology/view/10.1093/acrefore/9780190236557.001.0001/acrefore-9780190236557-e-166?print=pdf.

Psychology Today. "Burnout." Accessed September 11, 2020. https://www.psychologytoday.com/us/basics/burnout.

Stoeber, Joachim and Julian H. Childs. "The Assessment of Self-Oriented and Socially Prescribed Perfectionism: Subscales Make a Difference." *Journal of Personality Assessment* 92, no. 6 (2010): 577–585. https://doi.org/10.1080/00223891.2010.513306.

Wadsworth, Emma, Kamaldeep Dhillon, Christine Shaw, Kamaldeep Bhui, Stephen Stansfeld, and Andrew Smith. "Racial Discrimination, Ethnicity and Work Stress." *Occupational Medicine* 57, no. 1 (2007): 18–24. https://academic.oup.com/occmed/article/57/1/18/1553660.

CHAPTER 5

Career Research. "Social Cognitive Career Theory." Accessed September 14, 2020. http://career.iresearchnet.com/career-development/social-cognitive-career-theory/.

CHAPTER 6

Burnett, Bill. "Designing Your Life | Bill Burnett | TEDxStanford." TEDxTalks. May 19, 2017. YouTube video, 25:20. https://youtube.com/watch?v=SemHhon19LA.

Davidson, Adam and Alex Bloomberg. "The Tuesday Podcast: The Economics of Pursuing Your Dreams." December 14, 2010. In *Planet Money*. Produced by Nick Fountain, Alexi Horowitz-Ghazi, Darian Woods and Alex Goldmark. Podcast. MP3 audio. 22:09. https://www.npr.org/sections/money/2010/12/16/132063242/the-tuesday-podcast-the-economics-of-dream-pursuit.

Nguyen, Lena. "The Hardest Engineering Majors: A Detailed Guide for Overachievers." *College and Career (blog)*. Transizion, June 7, 2020. https://www.transizion.com/hardest-engineering-majors/.

CHAPTER 7

"10 professions with the best job security." MarketWatch, January 29, 2016. https://www.marketwatch.com/story/10-professions-with-the-best-job-security-2015-03-20.

Doody, Ryan. "The Sunk Cost 'Fallacy' is Not a Fallacy." *Ergo: An Open Access Journal of Philosophy* 6 (2020): 1153-1190. https://doi.org/10.3998/ergo.12405314.0006.040.

Gibson, Michael. "The Ivy League Has Perfected the Investment Banker and Management Consultant Replicator." *Forbes*, February 7, 2014. https://www.forbes.com/sites/michaelgibson/2014/02/07/the-ivy-league-has-perfected-the-investment-banker-and-management-consultant-replicator/#6a9f00d3178a.

Jubbal M.D., Kevin. "5 Happiest Types of Doctors." Med School Insiders, November 10, 2019. https://medschoolinsiders.com/medical-student/5-happiest-types-of-doctors/.

Pappano, Laura. "First-Generation Students Unite." *New York Times,* April 8, 2015. https://www.nytimes.com/2015/04/12/education/edlife/first-generation-students-unite.html.

CHAPTER 8

Cherry, Kendra. "Understanding Collectivist Cultures." VeryWellMind. Accessed March 24, 2020. https://www.verywellmind.com/what-are-collectivistic-cultures-2794962.

Hanas, Jim. "You Are Not Going to be Famous." *New York Post.* July 25, 2009. https://nypost.com/2009/07/25/you-are-not-going-to-be-famous/.

"I Quit Law School to Become an Actress | L.A. Land | Refinery29." April 14, 2018. YouTube video, 7:41. https://youtube.com/watch?v=vDzx72w_uU8.

Occupational Outlook Handbook. s.v. "Actor." Accessed September 25, 2020. https://www.bls.gov/ooh/entertainment-and-sports/actors.htm#tab-1.

"Yvonne Orji of 'Insecure' on Becoming a Comedian: 'My Mom Definitely Cried'." Associated Press. June 10, 2020. YouTube video, 2:54. https://www.youtube.com/watch?v=4T_kJCCYvRw.

CHAPTER 9

Breitfelder, Matthew D. and Daisy Wademan Dowling. "Why Did We Ever Go Into HR?" *Harvard Business Review,* July 1, 2008. https://hbr.org/2008/07/why-did-we-ever-go-into-hr.

Kuris, Gabriel. "How to Choose Between Applying to Law School, Taking a Gap Year." *U.S. News & World Report.* Accessed October 1, 2020. https://www.usnews.com/education/blogs/law-admissions-lowdown/articles/how-to-choose-between-applying-to-law-school-taking-a-gap-year.

Ngyuen, Tam. "Nailing the American Dream, With Polish." Interview by Karen Grigsby Bates. *All Things Considered*, NPR, June 14, 2012. Audio, 7:00. https://www.npr.org/2012/06/14/154852394/with-polish-vietnamese-immigrant-community-thrives.

Yakushko, Oskana, Autumn Backhaus, Katherine Ngaruiya, Megan Watson, Jaime Gonzalez. "Career Development Concerns of Recent Immigrants and Refugees." *Journal of Career Development* 24, no. 4 (Summer 2008): 362–396. https://doi.org/10.1177/0894845308316292.

CHAPTER 10

Brinson, Linda. "What is BigLaw, and why is it in danger?" Howstuffworks. Accessed September 6, 2020 https://money.howstuffworks.com/biglaw.htm.

Encyclopedia Britannica Online, Academic ed. s.v. "Confirmation Bias." Accessed September 5, 2020. https://www.britannica.com/science/confirmation-bias

Fines, Glesner. "Competition and the Curve." UKMC. Accessed September 6, 2020. https://web.archive.org/web/20061210031213/http://www.law.umkc.edu/faculty/profiles/glesnerfines/competition.htm.

Reeves, Arin. "Written in Black & White - Exploring Confirmation Bias in Racialized Perceptions of Writing Skills." *Nextions, (2014)*: https://nextions.com/wp-content/uploads/2017/05/written-in-black-and-white-yellow-paper-series.pdf.

CHAPTER 11

Carmichael, Evan. "No regrets - Jeff Bezos - Have NO regrets," Evan Carmichael. June 15, 2014, YouTube video, 2:59. https://youtube.com/watch?v=ikuLEZoE1vE.

Kane, Sally. "The Realities and Myths of Practicing Law." The Balance Careers. Last modified October 7, 2019. https://www.thebalancecareers.com/myths-regarding-the-practice-of-law-2164697.

Latham, Tyger. "The Depressed Lawyer." *Psychology Today*. May 2, 2011. https://www.psychologytoday.com/us/blog/therapy-matters/201105/the-depressed-lawyer.

Manson, Mark. "Why Some Dreams Should Not Be Pursued." *Mark Manson - Life Advice That Doesn't Suck*. Accessed September 16, 2020. https://markmanson.net/dreams.

O'Keefe, Paul A., Carol S. Dweck, Gregory M. Walton. "Implicit Theories of Interest: Finding Your Passion or Developing It?"

Psychological Science 29, no. 10 (September 2018): 1653-1664. https://doi.org/10.1177/0956797618780643.

Thomas, Eric. "Secrets to success Pt. 1." Etthehiphoppreacher. December 11, 2008. YouTube video, 9:01. https://youtube.com/watch?v=5fsm-QbN9r8.

CHAPTER 12

Botsman, Rachel. "I Don't Know What to Say." LinkedIn. Published June 15, 2020. https://www.linkedin.com/pulse/i-dont-know-what-say-rachel-botsman.

Caffier, Justin. "Comedians Reveal What the L.A. Stand-up Scene Actually Pays." Vulture, published June 20, 2018. https://www.vulture.com/2018/06/comedians-reveal-what-the-l-a-stand-up-scene-actually-pays.html.

Merriam-Webster. s.v. "plan (*n*.)." accessed October 5, 2020. https://www.merriam-webster.com/dictionary/plan.

Prisco, Jacopo. "Illusion of Control: Why the World is Full of Buttons that Don't Work." CNN. Accessed October 9, 2020. https://www.cnn.com/style/article/placebo-buttons-design/index.html.

CHAPTER 13

Burnett, Bill and Dave Evans. *Designing Your Life: How to Build A Well-Lived, Joyful Life*. New York: Alfred A. Knopf, 2016.

Plumer, Brad. "The Science Behind that Absurd Color-Changing Dress, Explained." Vox. Published February 27, 2015. https://www.vox.com/2015/2/27/8119901/explain-color-dress.

CONCLUSION

Pearl, Robert. "The Science of Regrettable Decisions." Vox. Published July 23, 2019.

CPSIA information can be obtained
at www.ICGtesting.com
Printed in the USA
FSHW021934201220